The Official Publication of the Series
LOUIS CHUNOVIC

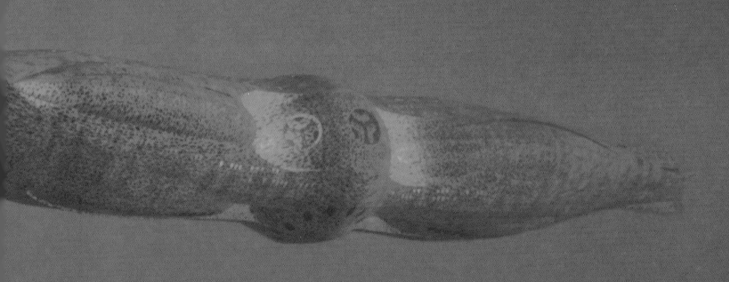

BOXTREE

First published in the United Kingdom in 1994 by Boxtree Limited,
Broadwall House, 21 Broadwall, London SE1 9PL.

Copyright © 1994 by MCA Publishing Rights, a division of MCA, Inc.

Photographs courtesy of Amblin/Universal Television
Design and colour reproduction by Blackjacks, London

ISBN: 0 7522 0978 7

A CIP catalogue entry for this book is available from the British Library.

Printed in Portugal

10 9 8 7 6 5 4 3 2 1

Contents

"I think that this is going to be *the* hippest show in about twenty-five years.

"I think this is gonna come back like *Brady Bunch*, *Star Trek* and *Gilligan's Island*.

"It's the kind of show that is, like, timeless; and people in 2018 are gonna go, 'Man! Is that what they thought?!'

"I think people are really gonna relate to this show in the future, and hopefully they'll learn a lesson from it, 'cause I think that we're teaching a lot of people now."

Jonathan Brandis

For Brian and Jesse Diamond,
who will be adults in the twenty-first century

ACKNOWLEDGEMENTS

seaQuest DSV is series television on a monumental scale, and writing about it has proven to be a monumental, albeit an engrossing, task as well.

The focus of the following relies heavily on active production participants, that is, those who stayed with the ship, both literally and figuratively. Certain important contributors to the show, especially Tommy Thompson and Rockne S. O'Bannon, are only glancingly included here. This book does not reflect the scale of their contributions and to them and to any others who may feel slighted, my apologies.

To the current crew – both in front of and behind the cameras: As you know best of all, this book was written during a tumultuous time, both for the show and for many of you – coping in the aftermath of the all-too-real Northridge earthquake.

My thanks for your many courtesies and my appreciation for your unfailing professionalism under tough circumstances.

INTRODUCTION
The Film Maker

"When I was a kid the one story that inspired me more than any other was *20,000 Leagues Under the Sea*. I used to pretend to be Captain Nemo and had a lot of undersea adventures with my Nautilus crew.

"I'd always wanted to explore the possibility of the depths of our oceans, as a stage, as theatre for all sorts of drama and science and entertainment."

So says Steven Speilberg, who through the vast array of films to his credit can unarguably be considered America's most prolific storyteller.

Without him there would be no *seaQuest DSV*, no undersea adventures of Captain Nathan Hale Bridger and his crew in the twenty-first century.

And without him, it's equally certain no network would have so eagerly rushed with a practically unheard of on-air commitment for twenty-two episodes [subsequently raised to twenty-four] of such a monumental, and monumentally expensive, project within twenty-four hours of hearing the pitch.

So it's here we begin. You will meet the boyishly enthusiastic creative executive whose life-long love of undersea adventure echoed Spielberg's own; the senior television executive who found ways to make the financially impossible feasible; the production designer who, one day, with little else to go on, was told to start thinking about submarines, and his colleague, who brought a surfer's love of the sea to the project; and the foremost underwater scientist who became the real-life model for Nathan Bridger.

Brace yourselves for a fascinating journey, capped by a week-long behind-the-scenes visit that begins with an earthquake in L.A. that seemed plucked right out of the imagination of our host. Life, like the show, you are about to discover, is full of surprises.

Welcome aboard, and don't forget

. . . Beneath the surface
. . . lies the future.

CREATING *SEAQUEST*
Philip Segal

The tall, friendly, boyish-looking fellow with a soft British accent and a wide-eyed, enthusiastic affinity is listed in the credit roll following each week's episode as the "executive in charge of production", and his official title is vice president of Amblin Television, the home-screen division of Steven Spielberg's production company.

But the truth is, all that's irrelevant alongside the single fact: *seaQuest DSV* is quite simply Philip Segal's baby.

Which is not to say he's not modest about the creation. Phil displays an absolute infectious charm and delight commensurate with a proud father showing you pictures of his one-year-old.

In his Santa Fe adorned office at Amblin, cluttered with fantastic toys, games, books and an abundance of scattered science fiction memorabilia, it's obvious to the visitor the man shares more than a slight similarity to the child-like nature of his employer. What better place to sit down and discuss the show's origins: *seaQuest* was developed internally, here at Amblin, by myself and Tony Thomopoulos (the president of Amblin Television).

The idea came from a couple of sources ... one, from the fact that Steven is a big fan of Jules Verne, especially *20,000 Leagues Under the Sea*. The Captain Nemo character is something that I think is indelible in his mind ...

That was the foundation. The rest comes from the fact that I grew up on sixties television – wonderful shows like *Voyage to the Bottom of the Sea, Lost in Space, Land of the Giants* and *Time Tunnel* – all of those wonderful creations from Irwin Allen. A little bit of his influence rubbed off on me. When you look at fantasy and adventure, you've really got to give Irwin a lot of credit for putting those things on television ...

Obviously, our ability to create better effects has improved through the years, but there was a sense of wonder to what he did. It's indelible, especially in the hearts of kids who loved science fiction, and I was one of them.

Richard Basehart, who starred in *Voyage to the Bottom of the Sea*, reminds me of Roy Scheider.
Very much so, very much so.

Was that conscious?

No, it wasn't ... The reason why Roy ended up being a part of this was simply because one of the things that we all sat around and talked about was the fact that television was lacking heroes, and we thought that it would be great to try to put some heroism back into the adventure. And he's a consummate actor, and there's very few heroic leading men that are available to us in television ... and he liked the arena.

Do you remember the first time you heard the word *seaQuest*? How far in the process was that?

That's a funny story. *seaQuest* was not the original title for this [show]. The original title for *seaQuest* was *Deep Space*.

While we were developing the show that was the title we used, and we thought it was a great title. And then of course, *Deep Space Nine* came out and we were forced to change the name.

We banged our heads against the wall for weeks trying to come up with a name. Finally we came up with *seaQuest* and we thought it was brilliant.

Then when we went into the title searches [a legal process to determine if a name has been previously or currently used or registered], we discovered that there was a French wetsuit company called Seaquest ... there was a cruise line called Seaquest ... there was a tuna company called Seaquest.

[Laughs]

... there was everything called Seaquest.

Did you have to deal with this?

Yes we did, we dealt with them. Everybody got dealt with.

[Laughs]

The funny thing is ... there were some people in very prominent positions – not Steven – who weren't crazy about the name *seaQuest*. They didn't think, really, it was meaty enough and bold enough, so we went on a search for a new name.

A company was brought in and the funny thing was that out of all the names they came up with, the one that tested most positive and that all the people felt was about the sea was ... *seaQuest*.

Do you remember the other names?

Oh. I remember the one they wanted to push on us: Salachian.

Meaning?

It's cartilaginous fish. It refers to sharks, rays, any fish in the ocean that is cartilaginous, with no bones, is salachian. They thought that was wonderful, and of course –

[Laughs]

we just didn't get it. So after weeks and weeks and weeks – we went out with a press release announcing the show with the name *seaQuest* and we didn't even own the title yet – but deals were made and *seaQuest* ended up being the title.

Why the lower case "s" and the upper case "Q", 'cause it looks good?

It looks wonderful ...

The original design concept was by Jim Lima [originally, the art director on *seaQuest*] ... James Lima is really the brainchild behind a lot of what you see; all the design is James Lima and Richard Lewis, our production designer (and Emmy winner for his work on *Max Headroom*).

But the reason why the upper "Q" [is there] is because icons are a very important part of the show. One of the things that we wanted to do was create a world in which we had military and science working together in the future. We had a vessel that represented the new United Nations, which in *seaQuest* is the United Earth/Oceans Organisation, and we felt we needed sort of its own cachet.

And so the upper case "Q" is really nothing more than a chance to service the shark [in the tail of the "Q"], which is the icon for Deep Submergence Operations, DSO, which is the body that designed and built the *seaQuest*.

If that's the first time you heard the word *seaQuest*, what about originating the concept of the show?

I went to Tony Thomopolous [Amblin TV president] and said, "Wouldn't it be wonderful to do a submarine show?"

"You know, *Star Trek* has conquered space, and yet nobody's really conquered the oceans of our world, our own space, since Irwin Allen did it twenty-five years ago. It's high time we had a show about us, about our future!"

We thought together that it would be a terrific idea.

Let's step back: you went in to Tony and said: Irwin Allen, submarine, near future ...

Right.

Then what happened?

He said to me, "Well, it sounds very expensive. I'm not sure it's doable. Go away," he said, "and see if you can come up with some ways in which we can do that world in a way that's feasible." And so one of the first things I did was investigate computer-generated imagery, which has become, really, the window to that world for us. I discovered that if we brought in our own facility, which we did, we could produce these very expensive-looking images at a very low cost ...

With Richard [Lewis], I began to investigate the possibility. When we realised computer-generated imagery was the right way to go, I put that building block aside.

Then I contacted Bob Ballard [the scientist and former naval officer, who is the model for Captain Nathan Bridger, as well as the show's technical consultant] ... who was in the Midwest on a book tour.

I got him at his hotel. I said, "I work for Steven Spielberg and I want to do an underwater show and you're the best guy to do it and I'm a huge *Titanic* fan [recalling the sunken luxury liner that Ballard located as well as pioneered the exploration of its remains] and whaddya think?"

He thought I was just another kook calling him. He said, "Send me some information," and so we started a dialogue ... I eventually went to his home ... we sort of became very good friends.

How did you know to contact him?

I'm very aggressive about going after elements I believe work for the show ... and I'm a *Titanic* freak.

I love the Titanic. I've read Ballard's books on the *Titanic* and I followed his exploits when he found the sunken luxury liner.

He was the obvious choice to make ... so I just cold-called him. I found where he was and I went after him ... and it's become a wonderful relationship.

What was his original input?

The original writer on the show was a gentleman by the name of Rockne O'Bannon ... He and I went back East to meet with Bob Ballard, who took us on nuclear-powered submarines and showed us around Woods Hole, the Oceanographic Institute in Massachusetts where Dr Ballard is the senior scientist of applied ocean physics and engineering. He gave us a really in-depth tour.

Then we went down to San Diego to Deep Submergence Operations.

He was instrumental in giving us a sense of what the world might be in twenty-five years if money was funnelled from NASA to the oceans of the world. If we had all those billions of dollars, what might we do?

And we took that as a blueprint and created the world of *seaQuest* based on his input.

My impression is that, unlike *Star Trek*, which violates the laws of physics all the time, *seaQuest* is strong on its science; that is, there's almost nothing in the show that's not either in the works, or plausible or existing.

Correct. That's very true. What we wanted was to create a world that we felt was plausible, and the reason why is the show's only set twenty-five years into our future, a future – God willing – you and I will see.

The sea is a very interesting place because you and I can go down to it, we can touch it, taste it, smell it and get into it ...

So, was Ballard a tough sell on this?

He was, he was a very tough sell for two reasons: first, he'd been approached by [director] Jim Cameron to do *The Abyss* and he was very excited until he got to page seventy-five in the script and there were little green men. That's when he passed on the project. I had to convince him that what we wanted to do is be true to the physics of the sea, and we didn't want to say, like *Star Trek*, that we're gonna visit strange alien worlds and meet aliens, but what we wanted to say was, that if a man moves into the ocean and begins to live in the ocean he's gonna take his problems with him.

There's gonna be crime, there's gonna be pollution, there's gonna be a population explosion, and how do we deal with those things? And so the heart of *seaQuest*, really, is the idea that a man, Captain Nathan Bridger ... had a vision that the future of mankind was not in space, but in the ocean. This show is really a window into his world.

Now there must've come a time when you and Tony marched into Steven's office and said, "submarine".

Yeah.

How was that? Tell me about it.

It was really at an interesting time because Steven was involved in *Jurassic Park* and thinking about *Schindler's*, but he was very excited about the possibilities of the show. Of course, he was in every pitch meeting [i.e. the meetings at which the show was "pitched" to the three networks].

Do you remember his original comment?

The first thing that came out of his mouth was really the comment about Captain Nemo, and the idea of being able to do a show that tapped into that world. He was very excited about it and the stories that could come out of that.

The show has that Disney-esque, *20,000 Leagues Under the Sea* feel to it.

Yeah, I think there's no sort of deliberate attempt to go after a certain image, but I really think it's the majesty of what was in the fifties, when *20,000 Leagues* came out. It was magical. And that book, the original book, I remember reading that when I was a kid ...

The ocean to me is still a very mysterious place ... it's more mysterious than space because it's so close to us.

Tony Thomopoulos

He's gracious, soft-spoken, and the first thing one notices about him is his full head of prematurely white hair. It might be easy to say he's earned it, given the depth and breadth of his background in show business.

Tony Thomopoulos, president since 1991 of Amblin Television, has been president of the ABC Network, beginning in 1978, heralding acclaimed shows such as *Taxi*. In 1983 he became president of the ABC Broadcast Group, which in addition to the network and its programmes, included a motion picture division, the ABC-owned television stations and a vast radio network. In 1985 he became president of Motion Pictures and TV Groups at United Artists; in 1986 the chairman of United Artists Pictures. Among the motion pictures he produced during his reign were *Prizzi's Honor, Rain Man,* and *Betrayed.*

When a visitor to his white-on-wood office at Amblin grumbles about gridlocked traffic in post-quake L.A., the enormously approachable Thomopoulos promptly outlines a zig-zagging route over the Hollywood hills to Universal Studios, where Amblin is situated, masterfully cutting the visitor's subsequent travel time in half. It's easy to imagine the same individual tackling budgets with the same care and expertise.

What exactly is the process by which an idea springs from somebody's head and becomes a TV show? My understanding is Phil Segal has a love of adventure – the sea – submarines.

And Jules Verne.

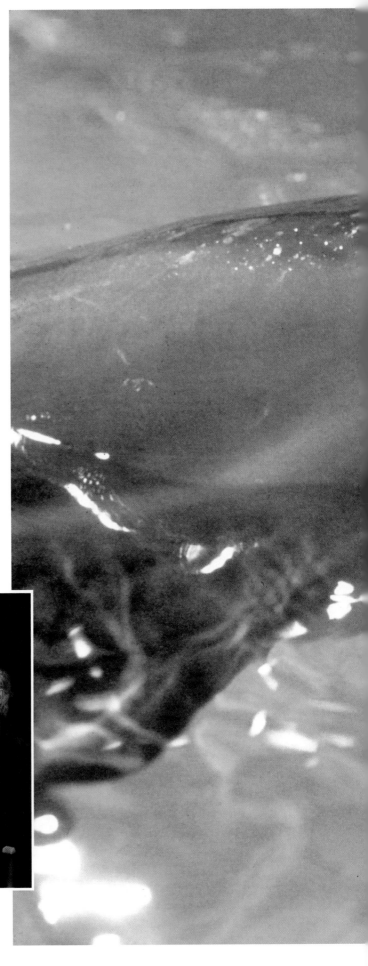

14

Right. So he comes in to your office and says, "What about a submarine show?"

Yes, that's true ... And we started a discussion about what kind of submarine it would be.

We started talking about maybe what would be *really* interesting would be something in the future, rather than current, and that the whole complexity of the world would change and so forth. And with that, Bob Ballard was called, and then from Ballard we decided to start building out and building on – getting the production designer, the art director and so forth and so on, and then finding someone who could write this and create a bible.

[A "bible" sketches recurring characters, explains the "arena" or setting, and outlines multiple themes or plotlines for a TV show.]

The way we've operated so far at Amblin is to create an idea, and from the creation of the idea to create a bible, and from the creation of the bible to create a presentation [to the networks, which are the buyers of proposed TV shows] ...

Once the idea germinated a while – we went around and around [about] what it was going to be. Ballard helped focus it a little bit for us, and Rockne [O'Bannon, a well-known television writer whose credits include Fox's *Alienation*, the *Twilight Zone* revival as well as Spielberg's own *Amazing Stories*] got involved and gave it some focus as well – and together we created this character called Nathan Bridger.

Then we went about the process of casting. The first person that came to mind was Roy Scheider. So we started putting the pieces together.

It was kind of a process of ebb and flow. It just kind of evolved as it moved along.

And what was your function in this? Was the first thing that went through your mind "too expensive"?

The philosophy, because of Steven and because of Amblin as a company, was to build a television series that was [to be] the core of the business; by that I mean, if the television show were successful, then let that show be spawning other businesses, such as toys, such as books, such as video games. Let your mind wander the tour attraction. Just let it go the whole gamut. A whole set of other businesses built around *seaQuest*.

So if you presented ... on that basis, that what you're looking to do is not just create a television show ... [to be on the air five years,

get into syndication and then make the studio a profit, then foreign distribution] the business has changed too dramatically ... So that if you can create that environment that allows these other businesses to explode, then the show is certainly not too expensive, and the gamble you're taking financially is pretty well within the parameters of a safety net.

So you don't need the sixty negatives or the hundred negatives any more?

You would like to have them, not necessarily because that's where you're gonna make your money, but because if you have sixty or a hundred negatives, that means you've been on the air three or five years, and if you've been on the air three or five

years that means you've got a known property that becomes a fixture in people's minds. So that instead of the *Back to the Future* ride they'll want to go to the *seaQuest* ride.

They're gonna go out and buy *seaQuest* toys, their kids are gonna want the dolphin and the plush toys ... They'll want to play the video game, they'll want to play the underwater submarine game.

But you don't really need the success on air? This is a new model of how to finance a TV show?

I don't think it's a model to finance a TV show, I think it's the TV show that allows you to get into other businesses.

For one, perhaps bad example ... car-washing. You take your car in to be washed, but you end up buying accessories for your car ... [Car-washing makes money, but] they're gonna make a lot more money in selling all those items to you. It's getting the customer into the store.

Think of the television series – and I don't want to use the term "loss leader", because that's not true – but as a leader to spawn other businesses. And the secret to it, the balance to it in my estimation – you can't do this with every television show, but if you're careful you can try to make the television series itself make a little money or break even. People say: "You spent all this money and you're gonna end up making one or two per cent?"

The answer is: "If that were the only reason you're doing it, it's probably not a good investment", but if you do all that and you make one or two per cent on the television programme, but you make ten to fifteen per cent on the other businesses, then it's a good business ...

The deficit [that is, the cost in which the studio absorbs over what the network pays] is understandable based on the potential of what the success of the show can be.

What was the pool of potential projects *seaQuest* was picked out of?

It's all in-house. We decided a long time ago ... because of the make-up of Amblin, that we would look at just a certain number of projects, a limited number of projects, and keep the development as small as possible ...

It was always *seaQuest*.

Once we made the decision that *seaQuest* was something we wanted to focus on, that's what we focused on.

And you said Roy Scheider immediately?

Because of the oceans and Steven's relationship with him [going back to *Jaws*] ... He was the right age, the right look ...

Then what? You had Roy, you had the bible, you had Ballard –

We had the production designers ... and then we called the three

networks and said we had a show and wanted to make a presentation ...

[And within twenty-four hours of hearing the presentation, NBC gave you a twenty-two episode on-air commitment, subsequently raised to twenty-four. This was a mammoth commitment for an untested one-hour dramatic series.]

Steven was very intimately involved in the sense that once we got our idea down, once we knew what we wanted to do and so forth ...

What was Steven's original input?

Steven liked the idea about the future and liked the idea about talking about the kind of world we'd go into – we would present a world of exploration and fantasy and there would be a heavy dose – as we call it – of science faction not science fiction. We talked about the characters, we talked about the direction of the series, we talked about a lot of aspects. And then as we started to write the bible, Steven saw what we were doing and got intimately involved.

I think we talked a great deal about Darwin with Steven, we talked about Bridger's character ... which was really more based on Bob Ballard.

We talked more about the world. Steven's input was about the world in the future, and what he wanted to make sure of was that we didn't present a negative image of the world. We didn't want to present a *Bladerunner* look at the world. We wanted to present the move to the sea as a positive step, and not as a reaction, a negative step ...

We figured that if we pushed the envelope further than twenty-five years, it would really fall into the category of science fiction and we really wanted to keep the science fact ...

What we're trying to accomplish now is to put more emphasis on character and have the stories generated from the characters rather than from outside events happening ... to have stories that are really generated by our characters.

Not taking away the adventure of the show, but rather than having the villain of the week or someone come and bring a problem on *seaQuest*, we want the problems to come out of our characters and our character relationships. That will make the show stronger.

The biggest message about this show is that it's like an embryo that had to grow. It is not a normal television show, it's a show that took a lot of direction finding itself, and it's still in the process of finding itself, because it's a show of such magnitude and size. [For example] no one ever attempted to do the kind of C.G.I. work [i.e. computer-generated imagery] we're doing. That in itself is an incredible story.

Richard Lewis

Bearded, baseball-capped, Richard Lewis leans back behind his cluttered desk in the office and smiles at a young illustrator who is bent over his drafting table. He smiles as if the man were working a cotton gin. Lewis allows that he does his designing on computers.

That duly noted, it's not surprising then that *seaQuest*'s original production designer won an Emmy in 1987 for *Max Headroom*, the sci-fi, TV-news-biz satire that was set "twenty minutes in the future": in both series, video in all its colourful, flashy manifestations is an important design element.

Lewis recalls that he was one of the very first to hear about the new series. He was on location in Atlanta filming the two-hour Civil War pilot *Class of '61*. It was, appropriately enough, a dark and stormy day ...

△ △ △ △ △ △

I was real miserable, it was raining, I had a temperature.

I was standing in a chow line with Phil Segal, one of the creative development people for Amblin, the one who was responsible for getting *seaQuest* started, and I think he detected I was a bit dejected and would've rather been anywhere else doing anything else at that moment, [so] he said, "Well, start thinking about submarines."

That was in February of two years ago [i.e. 1992].

Then what happened?

Four months later I got a phone call: "Have you been thinking about submarines?" I said, "Yah." And he said, "Come on in. Let's start putting it together."

Amblin is unusual in that it puts a production designer on at the beginning of development. Most television production companies hire a writer, go pitch it to the networks, get an order and *then* hire, somewhere along the line, a production designer to try to figure it all out in about six weeks.

But Amblin has been putting production designers on at the beginning of development along with the writer, up front.

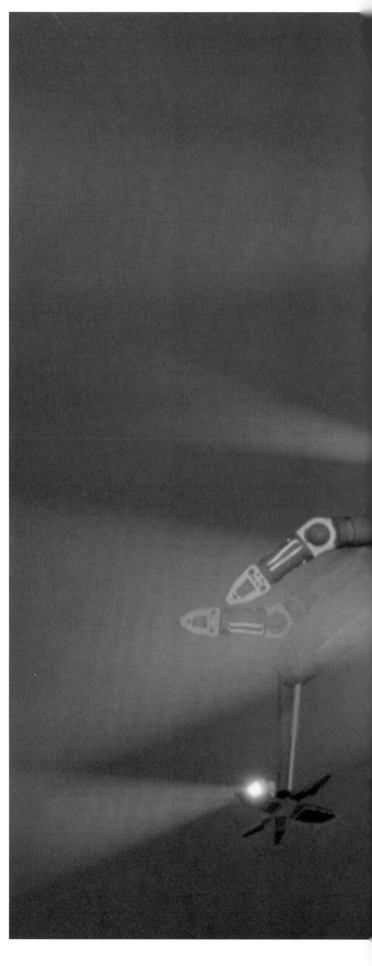

So what did you do for those four months?

I'd gone off and done another TV movie, and in the back of my mind I had thought about it and my first reaction when he said that to me was "I think it should be like a hammerhead shark," and hence the *seaQuest* logo is a hammerhead shark. The boat doesn't look like it [though].

When he asked me to come in and start putting it together, we hired an illustrator [Jim Lima], who had gone on to become my art director on the show once we got an order and a start-up, and is now the head of the computer animation department [at Amblin] also.

How did you two work together?

It was very interactive. He does brilliant illustration. I do not pretend to be an illustrator.

We would sit down and discuss what kind of images we wanted to create ... when I do illustrations at all, it's on a computer generally ...

Jim had been doing illustrations of the small craft, the shuttle, the pick trucks that the miners would have and weaponry, hand-held props, diving suits ... I was concentrating on the *seaQuest* itself ...

[But we] were very much partners in the initial design phase of *seaQuest*: our fingerprints are all over everything. There's nothing that's a hundred per cent him; there's nothing that's a hundred per cent me. As production designer I was responsible for ultimately producing the visual elements, but we worked as a team, we worked as a pair ...

One of the things that we needed [from the network] was a commitment of twenty-two episodes to be able to amortise the cost of development. We're creating a new world, we're creating a lot of sets and props, and things you just can't go down and get off a shelf ...

I think this was one of my major contributions, to convince Amblin that the only way to make the show producible was using computer animation instead of traditional miniatures. Traditional miniatures would be too limiting and expensive to produce on a weekly basis. Computers had gotten to the point where [they] could handle it, and that you didn't need high-end systems to accomplish it. You could do it on systems that humans can afford it.

What systems would that be?

Video toaster systems. Commodore Amiga.

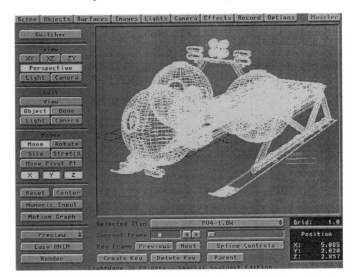

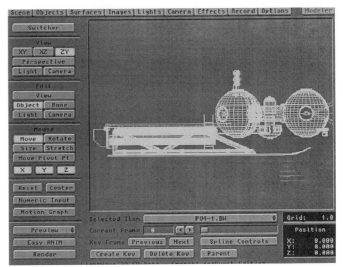

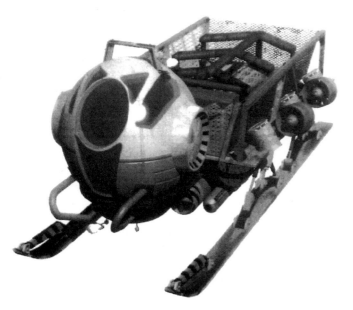

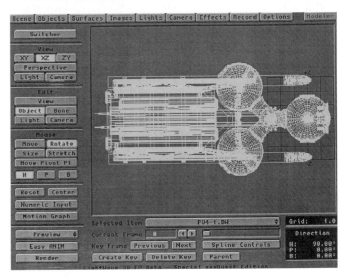

You couldn't have said affordable five years ago. When is the first time you could make that statement?

Early nineties ... The price of the computer system, for a person to go out and turn out film quality animation, has come down to in the five-thousand dollar range per machine.

And something else that it brought to us that was an interesting phenomenon, and that's that it wasn't just the computer systems that made that possible, but it's the talent of the animators that come off of the low-end systems ...

These are systems that individual animators have at home, and when you deal with the high end, you deal with Silicon Graphics and you deal with some work stations; in traditional computer animation houses, there are systems costing hundreds of thousands of dollars. So the people who work on them don't have one at home; they can't play. The machines cost so much money and the software costs so much money that they spend their entire workday cranking out corporate logos ... chrome letters, or television titling, or corporate I.D. work for commercials.

They don't get to play with the toy. They don't get to experiment with their own ideas. They're there to perform a service. It's hard to find a lot of animators coming from the high end that have done what amounts to photo-realism, that have done science fantasy, and on the low end you find people who have done it as a hobby for five or six years, and now the machines are fast enough to turn out quality work.

I've been playing with 3D animation as a pre-production tool since 1986, and used it on *Coming to America*, where I was art director, to show some blue-screen effects and to demonstrate a matte painting — a pan off a domed ceiling ...

Can you do photo-realistic computer animation on low-end machines?

We're doing it every week on *seaQuest*; it's all being done on Video Toasters.

So with five thousand I could set up and do *seaQuest* animation at home?

Technically, yeah. But the problem becomes scheduling – you can turn out the images on one five-k system – but to [properly] turn out the animation, you'll need many, many machines. It will be cheaper and more flexible if you do it on a low-end system than it will be on a high-end system, currently.

But it's getting very fuzzy-line in between them now, because the high-end systems have had to come down drastically in price, [and] low-end systems' capabilities have come up to where there's very little difference between the two.

I remember a time when only the Pentagon and George Lucas had these Cray machines – twelve-million-dollar monsters. Is there a purpose for those now?

We have a rendering module for *seaQuest* called the Screamer. It is twice as fast as a Cray I [was] and costs ten thousand dollars ... It's a rendering-accelerator for the Video Toaster ...

Was there a eureka moment in pre-production?

It isn't that cut and dry. It was a voyage of discovery. It was trying things. There were so many battles to be fought on so many levels and so many sets to do that you were never given the opportunity to just say eureka because it was one small element that you solved, it was never the total picture.

We had solved the total picture as far as a style.

What was that style?

It is tactile. We wanted to create a place where people physically had to work hard to do their job, that it was not just glowing panels that you put your hand over like in *Star Trek* and almost telepathically communicate with the console. We wanted something where you had knobs and valves and buttons to push, and things that would take energy to make it move ...

Secondly, we wanted it to be hydro-dynamic and bring that into the inside as well as the outside. We wanted the outside to be fishlike ...

In TV-land is *Max Headroom* happening on land, while *seaQuest* is happening in the water?

Max Headroom was twenty minutes into the future; we're twenty-five years ...

There are certain things that I like, that I tend to bring to a project: first of all, the pervasive presence of video technology.

I think in twenty-five years we'll have video-chip earrings that you'll programme some little animation on. I think there will be that sort of proliferation ...

There should be computer devices everywhere [on the show's sets, but] they needed to be practical. We couldn't burn them in like *Star Trek* does most of the time, because it limits the direction you can shoot. We wanted the freedom to move anywhere.

I wanted [the video screens] to appear as a letterbox format – a sixteen-by-nine, because that's the direction that television is going in already ... and they had to be flat screen not glass tubes, which is a real challenge since the technology isn't there to really do it really well yet. So we had to use video projectors as opposed to standard glass monitors ...

When you get into technology-based shows, the production designer has to think [about] more than just the aesthetic design of a show, but also how you bring that image to the screen every week, and it was sorting out what the options were for video graphics ...

We're past the point ... where audiences will accept roll bars scrolling through [in-screen video] like they did in the seventies, so you either have to produce everything at twenty-four frames, which means doing a lot of standard conversions, rendering out animations from the computer, transferring it to twenty-four frames, or using computers that do twenty-four frames, of which most of them don't handle animation very well ... or finding a way to do thirty frames that doesn't have a roll bar, and the way to do that is through LCD technology ... There's no roll bar at any speed.

Everything [on *seaQuest*] is [rear-screen] LCD projectors ... That [gives] us the ability to render everything at thirty frames and use off-the-shelf video components ...

The alternative is to do what *Star Trek* does, which is put up a transparency and then occasionally come in and cut up to a point of view of an animation. They seldom actually have a lot of playback.

The front one [on the *Enterprise* bridge set] is a blue screen and the side stuff are transparencies, or if there's any motion in it what they've done is taken and put a polarizing filter that rotates and reveals some things, but it doesn't have a lot of energy.

We wanted to be able to feed live video, to be able to switch live video, to be able to have somebody hit a button and bring up some graphic and have it turn into another kind of graphic, and have that kind of energy as part of the design inherent to the show.

The deep seas are far more dangerous than space ...

The differential of pressure between inside a space capsule at one atmosphere and outside a space capsule at zero atmosphere is one atmosphere difference. When you go into the deep oceans, the differential can be thousands of atmospheres difference ...

Also we wanted to make it a less than perfect place; you notice there's a lot of water dripping around door seals, especially in the launch bay – no matter how good things are, it's not perfect ...

The one thing we wanted to be the complete antithesis of *Max* is [that] we wanted it to be a positive future – not necessarily a safe future, but at least a positive one – that we have survived, that through some turmoil things have gotten somewhat better, but that people haven't changed.

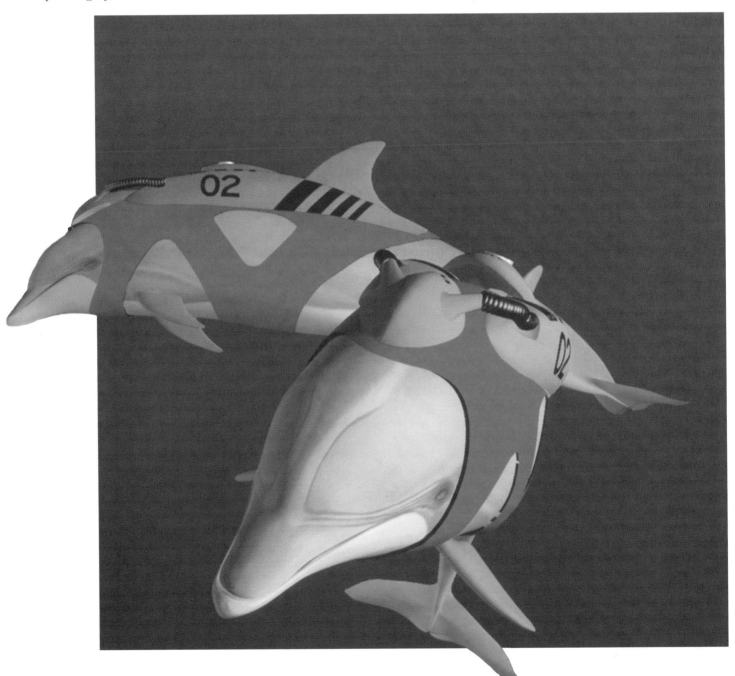

James Lima

Lanky, long-haired and amiable, James Lima was the original art director and conceptual designer on *seaQuest* and now is both the effects supervisor for the show and the director of Amblin Imaging, Amblin Entertainment's in-house C.G.I. shop.

The average *seaQuest* episode, he says, contains from seventeen to thirty C.G.I. shots – that is, computer-generated images – triple what was originally envisioned for the show.

Lima is a native Southern Californian and a self-proclaimed former surfer kid. Among his designs is the show's logo, the typeface of which is now trademarked. Its name: Limavetica.

What is a conceptual designer? And how is it different from an art director and a visual effects supervisor?

A conceptual designer is someone who's either brought in before there's a script ... or if someone just has an idea for a film or a television show. As a concept designer you kind of conceptualise the world [that] that film or television show will inhabit.

It goes as far as what the vehicles will look like or the costumes and props and things like that. You do an overall visual imagining of what this world will look like.

As an art director, you have to take all these ideas and put them into practicality and actually go through the process of ... making sure they can be built and what the colours are and then overseeing the set construction.

A visual effects supervisor is basically like a director. Instead of directing actors, though, I'm directing computer actors ... the whole of the computer world [including the submarine, the various vehicles, etc.].

All the shots you see in the show that actually show the outside water are in the realm of my responsibility. It's really like being a second unit director, [but] ninety per cent of the shots are really computer-generated; the other ten per cent are composites.

Amblin Imaging's first client is *seaQuest*. We are a visual effects company that primarily does computer work and

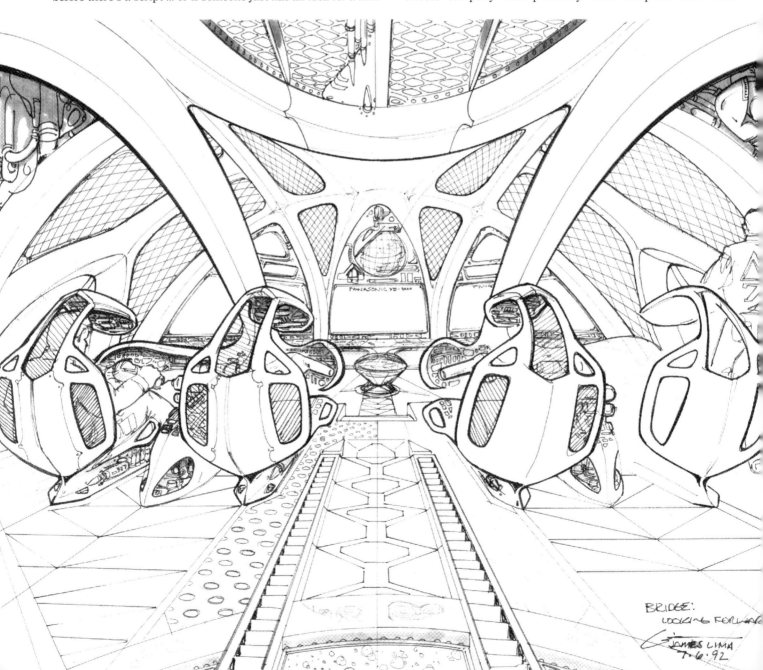

BRIDGE:
LOOKING FORWARD

James Lima
7.6.92

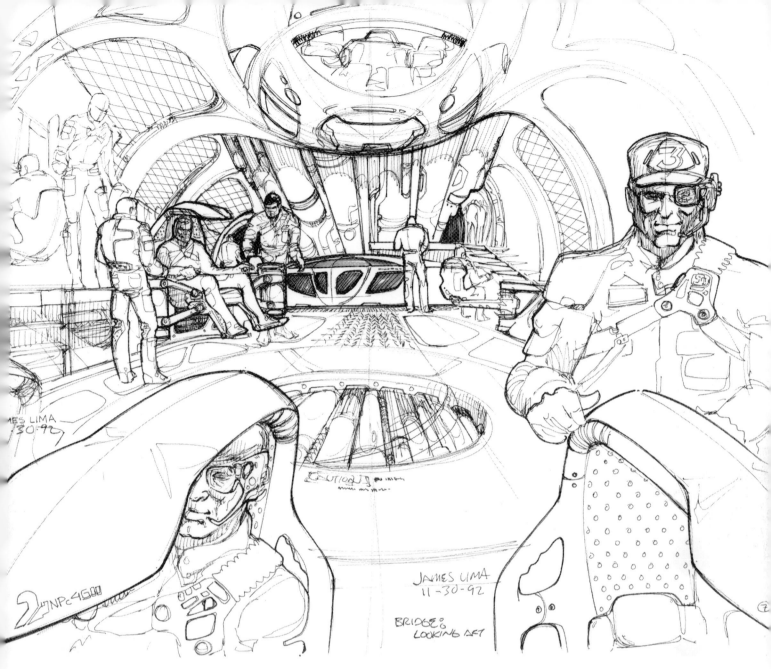

computer-generated imaging ... If we had to, we could also do miniatures.

How'd you get into this?

I went to work for General Motors. I wasn't designing cars, I was working in their Epcot Studio, which is future-world designs for transportation and environment, for the World of Motion Pavilion at Epcot Center in Disney World.

And Disney ... offered me a job back in California ... My first job was working with a great hero of mine, who's since become a good friend, Jim Cameron [director of the two *Terminator* films and *Aliens*, among others], and he was directing a theme-park ride and a film for Disney. [The film, *Time Vortex*, wasn't picked up out of development.]

I realised [from that] that what I really wanted to do was work in film.

I left Disney, I was in New York ... art directing commercials, and I got a call to go work on *Total Recall*, and the rest is history ... I was a visual effects art director on *Total Recall*.

You were on this project long before it was called *seaQuest.*

It was just called an underwater submarine show.

Before it was called *Deep Space*?

Oh yeah, this was in June ninety-two ... I was visual effects supervisor on this commercial for Pepsi International with Michael Jackson; very bizarre, surreal commercial, where Michael actually goes into his album cover, the "Dangerous" album cover ...

I got a call from Phil Segal, who's a vice president of Amblin Television, and [he] said that my name was highly recommended and he had this top-secret project that I might be very interested in, and when could we set up a meeting [so] I could show him my work. I always, always, *always* wanted to work for Amblin ... "to work with Steven!" He's always been a huge inspiration to me.

What is it about Steven that inspires you?

His vision, his creativity, the fact that he'll do the impossible ... They're always a year ahead of everybody else ... I admire that fearless quality that he has. He just does it. And on top of that, he's very articulate and very focused. Those are all the things I admire in a great artist, because he's able to release these images and these emotions that he has.

So you get this call from Phil Segal.

And I go in there, and about halfway through my portfolio he goes, "Okay, stop, you're hired," and that's the first time that's ever happened ... He was so taken by this one painting I had in there that I did for General Motors, which was a luxury yacht, a luxury ship, and it essentially never docked and it was a mile long.

It was kinda taking the idea ... Frank Lloyd Wright had of the mile-long building and then putting it out in the ocean. So I designed this very elaborate ship that had this upper deck that always stayed above the water and a lower deck that acted like a submarine. This kind of floating island was also this resort and also a manufacturer of things like fish products.

That was the image that started it, and interestingly enough the head of that ship is similar to the head of *seaQuest.*

Phil said, "Here's the deal, here's what we're doing.

"Steven wants to do an underwater TV show, kind of like an underwater *Star Wars*, this huge show that's never been done before, something like what we all kinda grew up with.

"You know, if you took like *Johnny Quest, Voyage to the Bottom of the Sea* and *The Thunderbirds*, the lunar shot and that whole kind of enthusiasm that the late sixties and early seventies had about the future and about creativity, and kind of lump it all together in one show. Well, that's what the show is about."

So the next three to four weeks was a very intense, very intense time, where we had like a million things to do during the day. We were inventing *seaQuest*, putting it together in a book; a *seaQuest* kind of bible.

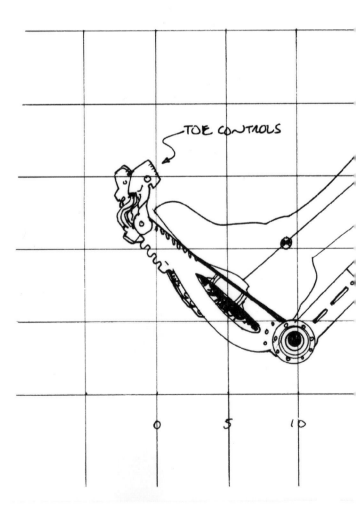

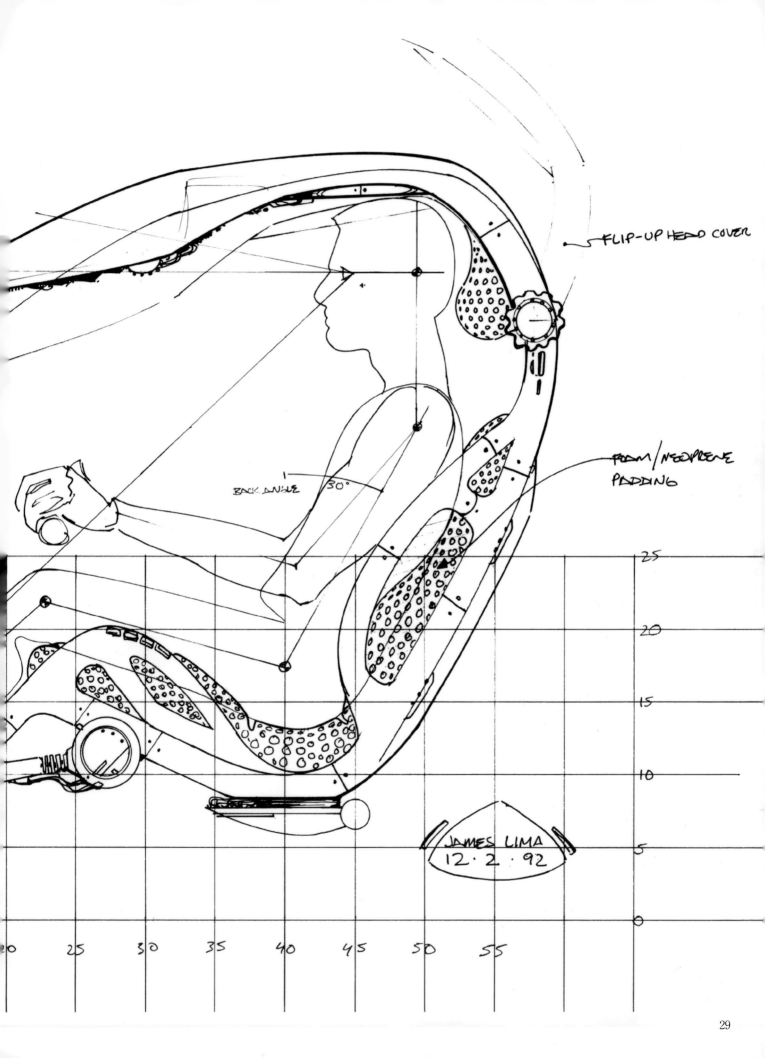

FLIP-UP HEAD COVER

FOAM/NEOPRENE PADDING

BACK ANGLE 30°

JAMES LIMA
12·2·92

25
20
15
10
5
0

20   25   30   35   40   45   50   55

HITCHCOCK
W/ "HR PROBE-
GEAR"

HEAD SET/VISOR &
GLOVES

JAMES LIMA
3·1·93

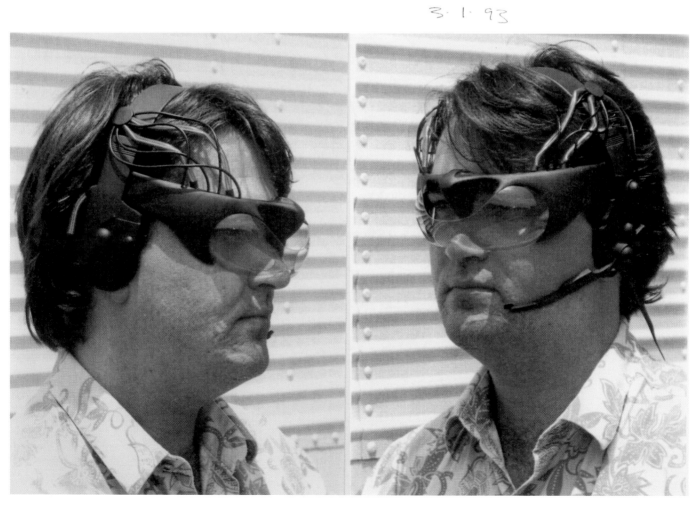

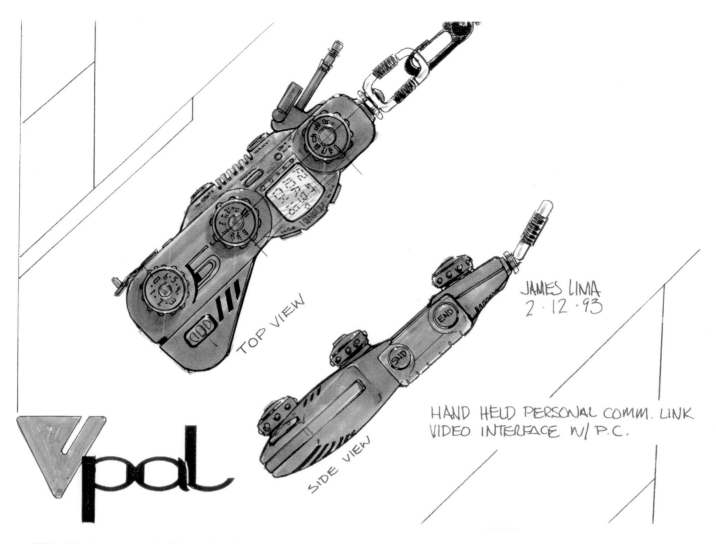

JAMES LIMA
2·12·93

HAND HELD PERSONAL COMM. LINK
VIDEO INTERFACE w/ P.C.

TOP VIEW

SIDE VIEW

Vpal

With this document and all these drawings ... I've done over a thousand sketches for *seaQuest* ... it was really fun, because the scripts were written and the story was evolving at the same time the images were evolving. The ideas could then blend and organically interface with how the stories would work, and the stories would come back and inspire a drawing.

What was the first image you created? Did they come to you with images or ...

No, they basically said, "We have to design the inside of the sub, we have to design the outside of the sub, how is Darwin gonna look?" ... That's how I came up with the [dolphin] rebreather ...

The very first image was the helmsman chairs, which are these kind of articulated, cocoon-like chairs ... on the bridge.

That organic kind of quality, what I like to call now nautical nouveau or hydro nouveau, the feeling of it is very much like the French school of art nouveau, except the lines are a little more taut, they have a little more snap to them ... From those things grew the bridge, which is in effect a cathedral. We have these flying buttresses and it's all saying, We're pushing back the pressure.

I wanted to design an environment that was impossible. The films I'd worked on, no matter how big the budget, we

were always stuck with, you know – here's a vertical, here's a horizontal, here's a simple curve.

The approach I took ... was a vehicular architecture, and it's quite different. So the idea was that the only thing that would be a straight line in that set, on the bridge, at all was the floor. Everything else flowed and was organic; it was the signature of the show... Even to the smallest props, everything has a curvilinear line to it.

Again like a cathedral, the playback screens or video screens or computer screens, the colours of them – which I supervise – the colours are like stained glass windows.

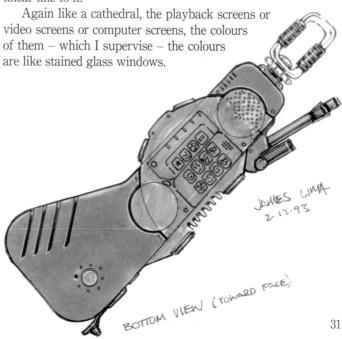

JAMES LIMA
2·12·93

BOTTOM VIEW (TOWARD FACE)

"DOCKING BAY"

12·30·92

CAST RIBS (HELMSMAN) FROM BRIDGE / FLACK SUITS FOR SECURITY / TRI-COLOR UNIFORM

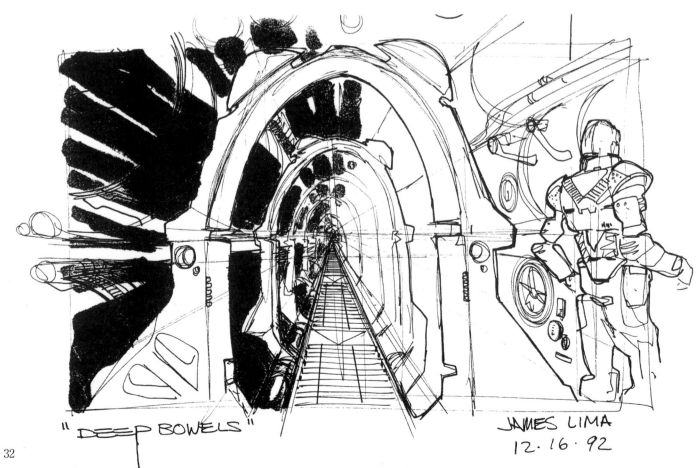

"DEEP BOWELS"

JAMES LIMA
12·16·92

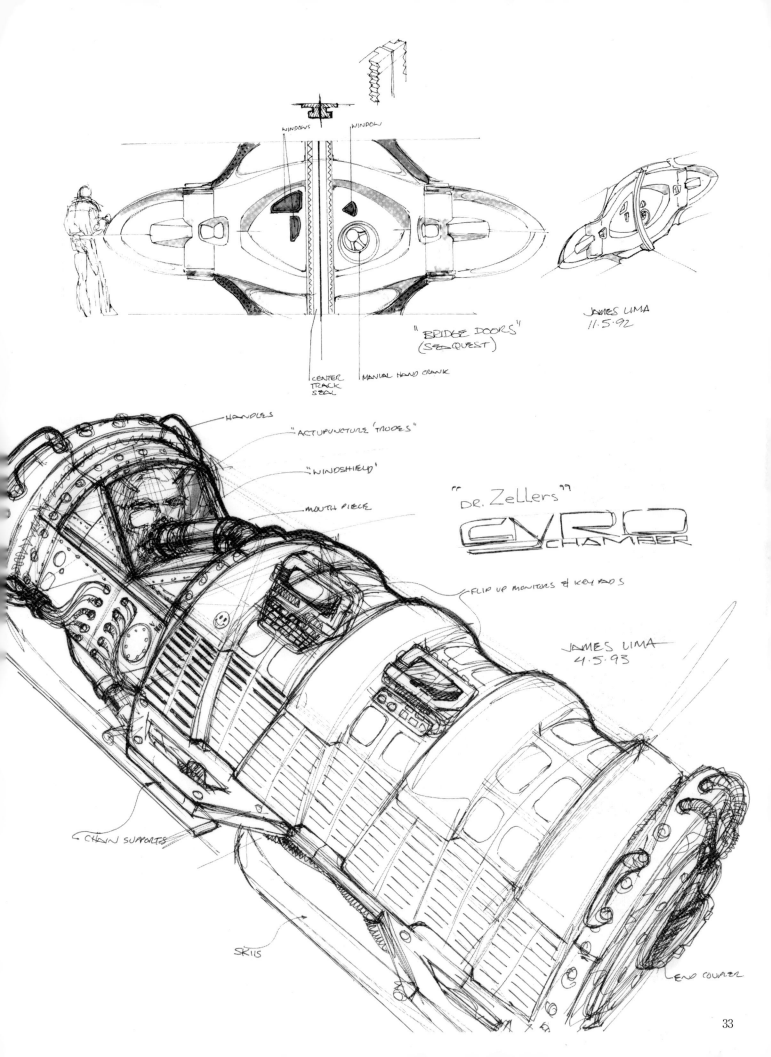

WINDOWS   WINDOW

"BRIDGE DOORS"
(SEAQUEST)

CENTER
TRACK
SEAL

MANUAL HAND CRANK

JAMES LIMA
11.5.92

HANDLES

"ACTUPUNCTURE 'TRODES"

"WINDSHIELD"

MOUTH PIECE

"DR. ZELLERS"
GYRO
CHAMBER

FLIP UP MONITORS & KEYPADS

JAMES LIMA
4.5.93

CHAIN SUPPORTS

SKIIS

END COUPLER

33

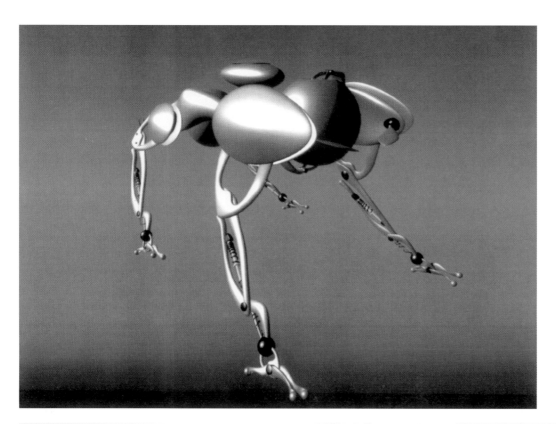

The blue and the amber?

Absolutely. I always feel that in great design art you have a duality of male and female shapes and forms and feelings, and if you put over that the connotation of the spiritual, even in the most subtle way, it takes on a very ... powerful presence.

I always felt that the bridge should have this very powerful presence. All great sculpture has this, whether it's Ferrari or a Bernini sculpture or a Michelangelo. They all carry in their weight and their mass and proportion those beautiful integrations between male and female shapes. And so, just about every vehicle you see in *seaQuest*, especially the *seaQuest* submarine itself or the Stinger or the Speeder, they all have these very male and female shapes to them.

How did you actually design the shape of the submarine?

Every once in a while you have these breakthroughs that happen. You're going along, then all of a sudden one day the design will just tell you ... It says, "This is what I am", and it presents itself to you.

Boom! And it suddenly became clear to me that the thing wanted to look like a squid – that the head in effect was the nose of a bullet, or the nose of a rocket, and that the rest of the vehicle was what air or water would do to that shape.

And so, you have this piercing, shovel, arrowhead shape in the front, and the back of it is just the effect of what that thing would do going through the water. When I design something, I'm very much intuition-driven; when I get a feeling about something, I just trust it and keep going ...

There are these male and female shapes in there [in the design of the sub] – there're muscles and mass, and that's Arnold Schwarzenegger's bicep right there next to Sharon Stone's hips. It was very exciting.

How did Bob Ballard fit into this?

Bob is a reality check. He's very inspirational ... a lot like Steven in that he's got the imagination and enthusiasm of a child or a young person, but with the knowledge and the experience of an adult. Again, there's a duality thing ... he set the parameters of the show; he said, "This is what happens in reality", and we have to be really respectful of that.

What's the most fun designing?

I would say it's definitely between the *seaQuest* and the Stinger.

The Stinger's a really cool story ... The idea behind this vehicle was that the tail would move. It's a one-person vehicle, very small, not unlike a formula-one race car ... This tail would allow it to move through the water, like a shark propels itself through the water ... The whole idea behind this was an underwater hotrod, an underwater motorcycle ... It's underwater signature would absolutely be stealth.

Bob saw that and he wanted a computer model ... and apparently now the military's building one. It's very exciting. I just hope they don't use it to bomb somebody or blow something up. I think that's the strength of science fiction, what Arthur C. Clarke did with satellites [i.e. imagining geosynchronous-orbiting satellites years before they were built].

What do you want the show to do that it hasn't done yet?

If it was up to me, I guess I would like the show to deal a little more with the mystery and the magical quality that the ocean has. There's the sense of poetry that I always add into the visual effects ... whether it's in really deep water and you get that lonely, cold feeling, or in shallow water where you can actually see the surface and little fish swimming by.

I grew up in the ocean, I've surfed for over twenty years now and there's something that happens to you when you go out ... When you leave the continent and step out into that ocean, you're in a different place, you're in a different world. You're in effect in as different a world as space is.

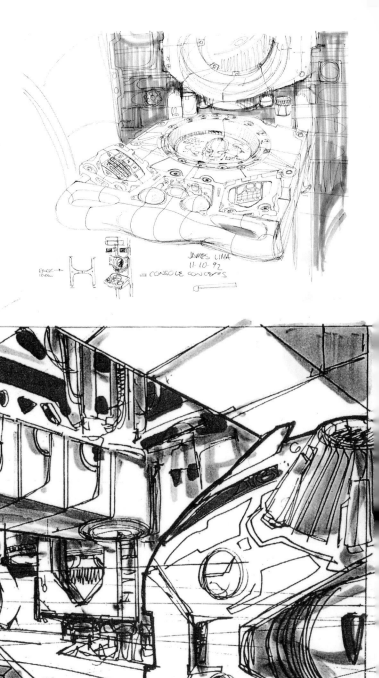

JAMES LIMA
11·10·92
CONSOLE CONCEPTS

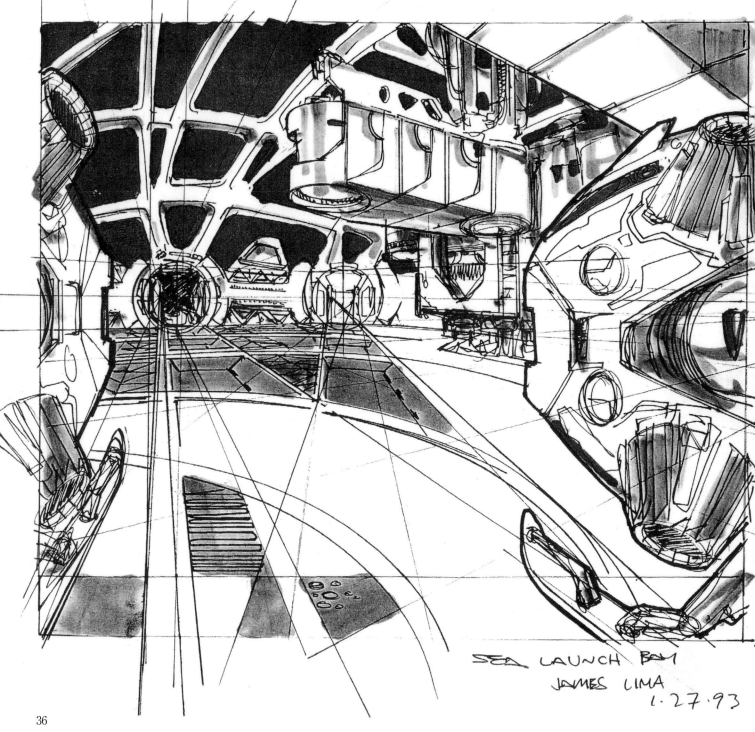

SEA LAUNCH BAY
JAMES LIMA
1·27·93

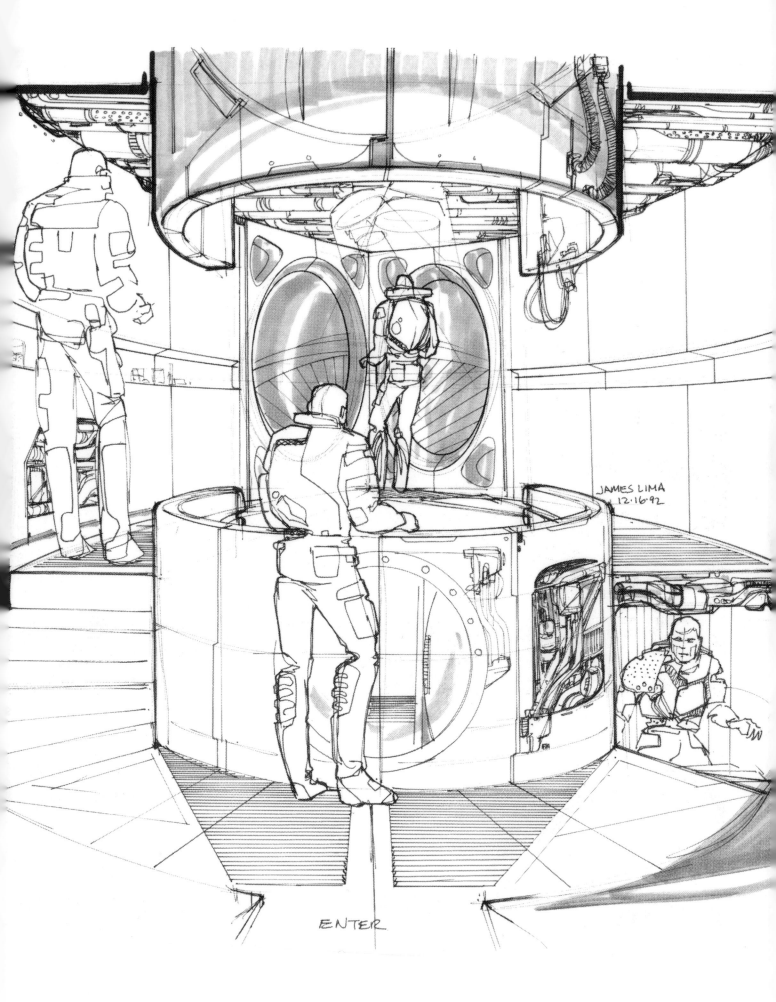

JAMES LIMA
12·16·92

ENTER

THE SCIENTIST
Robert Ballard

Production designer Richard Lewis called it "one of the most fun parts" of creating *seaQuest*: the opportunity to "interact and talk ideas" with the show's eminent technical consultant, Doctor Robert Ballard.

"Doctor Ballard wears many hats and is very knowledge-able of so many areas of exploration of the deep sea," the designer says, "design of naval equipment, naval espionage.

"He has his hands in much of the later twentieth century. He's this walking storehouse of that information, and as a scien-tist can express himself in ways that you don't generally find out of a traditional naval tech adviser. His earliest contribution was that the *seaQuest* should somehow reflect a fish-like shape, that in order for submarines to go fast they will have to do that.

"That was the real ... eureka and it was really early on." But that was only the beginning of Ballard's contribution to the show.

The oceanographic researcher's résumé is as staggering as it is impressive. With doctorates in marine geology and geophysics, the former intelligence officer and submarine commander is an acclaimed author and undersea explorer. He not only discovered but pioneered the exploration of the famed ocean liner *Titanic* as well as the German battleship *Bismarck* in their watery graves. Currently, he occupies the seat as senior scientist for the depart-ment of applied ocean physics and engineering at Woods Hole Oceanographic Institute in Massachusetts. Also, he just so happens to be the model for Captain Nathan Hale Bridger.

And that's still not all.

Ballard appears at the end of each episode almost as a latter day *Mr Wizard* supplying a brief science-fact addendum to each story.

Because he knows each script "cold", as he puts it, Ballard writes those end-of-episode moments himself, and because his wife is a television producer they're in-house productions in every sense.

Ballard also critiques each script – preferably before it shoots, but critique he does regardless. His on-point comments would almost fill a volume themselves. The following is just one sample from his remarks about the script for the episode titled "Hide and Seek", in which William Shatner guest-starred. [For more on the filming of "Hide and Seek" see the section herein called THE SHOOT.]

"General comments dealing with the flooding of *seaQuest* to go deep. The basic idea goes as follows. All of the compartments in *seaQuest* were not designed to go too deep (20,000 feet) since the only shape that works at great depth is a sphere. There are, however, several spherical compartments in *seaQuest* where people can go when a deep dive is made. The rest of the sub's compartments are then flooded with water. So far, we have only shown one of these spherical compartments working, that being the Bridge which has large clamshell doors and reinforced ribbing inside. We can imagine that there are several other spherical compartments within *seaQuest* like the Bridge where people go for a deep dive. They would include the sleeping areas, engine room, science labs, mess deck and other areas where a lot of personal gear and delicate equipment is found that cannot stand pressure and immersion in seawater. The most likely compartments to flood are all the passageways, the Maglev, large general work areas, etc."

Whether he's correcting a script writer's geography ["The Caribbean Sea is south of the US not west of Cape Hatteras. Perhaps you could say south of Puerto Rico"] or supplying the proper nautical jargon ["The word 'rope' is never used at sea. Rope is called a line at sea but in this case they would be using a cable – i.e. a strong line with steel in it."], Robert Ballard is *seaQuest*'s *DSV*'s reality check, their line of legitimacy.

Why don't we start at the beginning. Tell me the first time you heard about the project.

My secretary got a phone call from [Amblin executive Philip Segal's office], trying to get a hold of me. And they simply said that they worked for Steven Spielberg and they were trying to start a new show dealing with under the ocean, and would I call. I get a lot of crazy phone calls.

That's what you thought this was?

Yeah ... I can remember once my secretary got a phone call and the person said, "This is the White House calling." And she went, "Yeah, sure." "The President wants to have dinner with Doctor Ballard." And she said, "Yeah, sure. Who else is going to be at the dinner?" "Well, the Prince and Princess of Wales." "That's just great. Why don't you just send an invitation." She hung up ... and it turned out to be true, and I went to the White House and had dinner with the Prince and Princess of Wales.

When the phone rings, we have no idea if it's going to be the White House or some wacko. When I found the *Bismarck*, some neo-Nazis were going to kill me for desecrating the grave, which I didn't do ... So, naturally, my secretary is sort of hard.

[But] she transferred me to Phil in his car and he began telling me about this new project ... They hadn't presented it to NBC at this point.

What did he tell you?

He said that he was a fan of mine, because he had been a *Titanic* buff, and Phil ... was raised in England, and he'd had a tremendous interest in the *Titanic*, and he'd followed my career.

He said that, basically, they wanted to do a mix of my background, which was as a naval officer and as a scientist, and then he went on to describe Bridger, that Bridger was going to have this similar background of part naval officer, part oceanographer, and that they were looking at convincing Roy Scheider, who had not agreed at that point, to do the show.

It ended up that I was going to be in San Diego a couple of weeks later at a submarine base ... In fact, I invited [Phil Segal] onto the submarine base to show him some of the nuclear submarines and deep-diving vehicles ...

[We talked for] hours and hours about what it could be like, what the future could be like in two thousand eighteen – what the technology could be like, what *seaQuest* could be like.

I told him about the vehicles we were developing that are called Autonomous Vehicles, which are in essence the WSKRS [i.e. Wireless Sea Knowledge Retrieval Satellites]. We talked about JASON [a remotely operated vehicle system that goes to twenty thousand feet, using fibre optics and broadcast-quality video imaging], which is in essence the hyper-reality probe ...

I'd also trained dolphins in Miami – for academia as well as for the military, and knew a lot about dolphin capabilities. We'd worked a lot on speech converters, on the ability to transfer the dolphin's frequency into our frequency and develop a two-way communications. And so, on and on it went, and he wanted to know if I'd be technical consultant to the show.

Did you meet Steven?

I met Steven after we'd already started working on the show, 'cause he was off in Hawaii at the time finishing *Jurassic Park*.

What did he ask you, and what did he tell you?

Well, he had similar – I mean, my childhood hero was Jules Verne's *20,000 Leagues Under the Sea*'s Captain Nemo, and evidently he'd had a similar, you know, feeling about that novel.

I mean, I looked at it as sort of a marriage of reality and fantasy, which is the way Steven's looked at it, that *my* job was the reality job and his job was the fantasy job, and the question was to weave those two elements into the programme.

Well, how do you think they've done?

It's very difficult for people to master this world ... I would say that the one who's mastered it the most has been [writer] David Kemper. The first one we did together was "Treasures of the Mind", which I think was a great show. "Bad Water" was a great show. The nice thing about David is that he'll call me at the beginning [of the writing process] and we'll kick it around. That's when, I've found, I can do the most good ... as opposed to being a policeman on the other side.

Tell me about both parts.

Well, the way [David Kemper] scripts out a show is to put it up on a bulletin board, and he has the tease, four acts and sixteen scenes – four major scenes per act – and an A-story and a B-story. I tend to concentrate on the A-story, because that tends to be ... dealing with the ocean; the B-story tends to be dealing with, you know, the interpersonal thing.

I'll give you an example of the way it worked on "Treasures of the Mind": he said, "We wanna do something on the Library of Alexandria, something about making a major discovery about it." And I said, "Well, you know most of it caught on fire."

This is when Julius Caesar attacked Egypt and they fought the Egyptian navy off Alexandria ... and [a burning ship] ignited the Museum of Alexandria, which was considered one of the greatest losses of all time ...

So I said, "Look, it's on the ocean. What if they had a customs house." Recognise that most of what came into the museum came from other countries. So imagine: they're going to have a bureaucracy back then. Assume that right on the ocean was a customs house; the ships would've been bringing in the great art and the great manuscripts, and they would've been processing them ...

Well, we know that that area can have earthquakes and we also know that earthquakes can cause what's called "liquefaction" of the ground ... So I said, "Let's have an earthquake and let's have this [customs house] just vanish [underwater] and let's have a big dome in it so that it can [be] airtight." And on we went ... He was able to build a whole story around that [basic premise] ...

You try to put [the story] in some sort of basis that is at least plausible, that isn't breaking the laws of physics.

When have you had to be a policeman?

For example, I would say the one I'm doing right now ["Abalon"], where they had [Commander] Ford diving to thirty-five thousand feet, and they were diving under ambient conditions. Well, he'd be dead. Absolutely no way that you could do that ... And they also wanted a chamber where there was a big air passage at thirty thousand feet. There's no way!

They were having Ford in the suit at thirty-five thousand feet experiencing nitrogen narcosis. In the first place deep diving [breathing] mixtures don't have any nitrogen in them, 'cause it'll kill you. So it can't be that. Plus, there's no way a person's gonna be at ambient pressure with eight tons per square inch on their body. Not a chance!

So I said, "Make it into a one-atmosphere breathing suit, and instead of having nitrogen narcosis have it be CO_2 circulation, have it be a poor circulating system that's causing a CO_2 build-up, and that can cause him all sorts of problems."

So my job is to take a situation and turn it around to where it has a degree of plausibility ...

He had a mermaid down there at thirty thousand feet. Can you imagine! I said, "What?! A mermaid!" And then he had the mermaid blowing bubbles. And I said, "In the first place the mermaid wouldn't blow bubbles. She doesn't have lungs, she has gills ... Let's say they do have different breathing systems, like some of the earlier amphibians ... where they can breathe in both air and water ... That means that when she leaves the surf and walks out of the ocean, she has to regurgitate, she has to clear her lungs — she has to spit out a lot of water, like she was

a drowning person." Well now, there it is, they're going to do that. They just had her walking out of the surf saying, "Hi, how the hell are ya?"

It strikes me that a difference between this show and, say, *Star Trek* is that built into *Star Trek* are elements that violate the laws of physics –

Right. All over the place. "Beam me down, Scotty." Right.

Every single episode must be an affront to a scientist.

Oh yeah.

In *seaQuest*, though, that's the exception, and the rule is: what you see on the screen is either something that's plausible or that's real.

Well, some episodes are and some aren't, and it's a question of where they ultimately want to take the show. If they want to take the show more towards *Star Trek*, that's fine. My job is to try to interject as much reality as the situation will permit, understanding that sometimes I win and sometimes I lose.

Well, what's your track record, what's the percentage?

I'd say it's pretty good. The vast majority of corrections that I put in, get in.

What're some of the technical things you've put in we wouldn't know about as viewers at home?

Well, you're going to see a show coming up ... the whole internal flooding [of the submarine] to go on deep dives.

The whole thing with Stinger. Stinger is based on research we're going at Woods Hole/MIT on how it is that fish can swim as fast as they do for the amount of energy they expend. That's because fish, by wagging their tail, organise their turbulence ...

What do you want the show to do that it hasn't done yet?

I want it to deal with future colonisation of the sea. See, the biggest problem with the show now is that the submarine can't surface. They don't really have an opportunity to show where most humans are going to be in the ocean: they're not going to be under it, they're going to be *on* it. They're going to be living in houses or habitats in the sunlit area. Most human habitation in the future is going to be zero to six hundred feet, and if you drain the ocean to six hundred feet you get an area of twenty-seven million square kilometres – the size of North America. Twenty-seven million square kilometres of sea floor feels the sun!

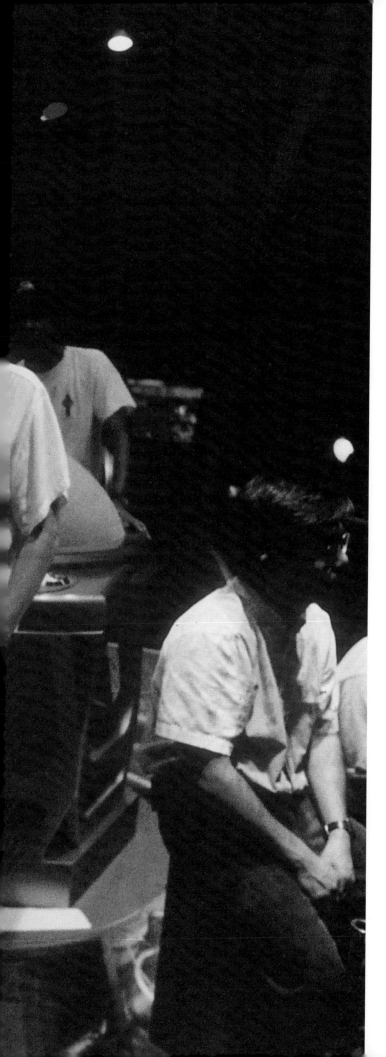

PAINTING WITH LIGHT
Kenneth Zunder

In series television, it is common practice to hire a different director for each new episode. It is the responsibility of the director of photography, or D.P., to give the production it's unifying eye.

Creative, even visionary, input at early stages of the process is one thing, but once the whole grand, unlikely machinery of week-in and week-out TV production is switched on, control passes to the front-line troops, and at the helm is usually the D.P.

"You prep [prepare one episode] while you shoot [another]," says *seaQuest*'s director of photography, Kenneth Zunder. "There's basically zero downtime."

Previously, Zunder was D.P. on *Thirtysomething* and *Brooklyn Bridge*. His vision on both series was recognised with award nominations from his peers, the American Society of Cinematographers, who also gave an A.S.C. nomination to his work on the *seaQuest* pilot.

What does a D.P. do before day one on a series?

Works with the production designer and the producers.

I was on before the director [of the two-hour pilot episode] was hired, and we do things like decide on technical things as well as artistic things – how do you want walls to fly, which walls are wild [in other words sets that can be quickly disassembled to accommodate the camera].

Before the sets are even built, we go over the plans with the production designer and the producer on what kind of look the show wants to have ... Directors come and go but the production designer, the D.P. and the producer stay, in order to maintain some sort of consistent look from episode to episode.

Stylistically, it may change a little from director to director: some directors might like longer lenses, some directors might like wider lenses, but you always want the bridge to look like the bridge, unless there's a special circumstance like power failure or battle alert, things like that.

So you work with the production designer and the producers, and you decide on a general kind of feel for the show ... as well as the technical things.

You work with grip and electric, key grip and the gaffer: where do we want to hang lights, how do we want to light this, do we need to hollow out a wall here so we can hide some cable?

Logistically, you want to work out where you're gonna put your lights with the technical people; and stylistically, you want to work out with the producers and the production designer the look of the sets, and you also want to work out the look of the actors – you wanna talk about wardrobe tests, make-up tests, hair, the dolphin ... water, what kind of feel you want for the show.

Did this show present any special problems?

Yeah, big time. We started this in March [of '93]. It was December before I did a shot with sunlight coming through the window ...

These sets are basically, from my standpoint, practical locations. On most sets, all the walls move, the ceilings move, you can cheat things here, there and everywhere.

[here] the pool doesn't move, the walls don't move, the big door doesn't move; on the bridge you have three different levels, all of which you have to work around. If you were on a set that you build for a normal show, you just [say] "Move the stairs out, we need to get the camera here."

Because we're on a set and the set is [supposed to be] underwater, I do several things to remind the audience that we are in fact underwater, and one of the things is, wherever possible, incorporate water into the shot, whether we see water behind people ... or create water effects on the walls.

We have underwater lights. We create that rippling [water] effect on the walls, reminding people of water, [so it seems] you're not on a soundstage but on a real submarine.

What else do you do to get that effect?

People associate blue with water, right? So a lot of areas of the set we'll light blue ...

So it's a combination, you know, of showing water, using blue light, things like that ...

One of the other things I do is try to create different environments inside the sub. It's such a large sub, it's almost like a self-contained city, so you don't want all the sets to have the same character to them ...

The bridge set is a harder look [than the water-pool sets]; it's colder, steel, metallic. That's where they're going to be at battle stations, if anywhere. It's more of a military environment.

We try to make all the sets look as different as if you were on a normal show, where you were in someone's living room and you were in somebody's kitchen, then in an office building, then you're in a park – we try and do that all within the confines of the sets here.

What else can you tell me about the consistent look of the show?

What we typically do, we take advantage of, like in the bridge set, it's a hard ceiling, so it's nice to show a hard ceiling.

Very rarely on soundstages do you have sets with hard ceilings. You have four walls with maybe a muslin ceiling or no ceiling ... so you would rarely have the camera low, photographing the ceiling. Also a lot of actors and actresses don't like to be photographed low, they feel it's unflattering; whereas I feel because this is part military, part science, the military half lets me get away with a little more dramatic look.

I like to move the camera, I feel that moving the camera involves audience more ... If you move the camera, you draw the audience in.

One of my jobs, as I see it, it to help tell the story visually ... I want to make [the audience] an active participant, instead of just an observer.

How many script pages do you average shooting a day?

Yesterday we did seven pages, forty-three set-ups. An average day is probably six pages, and we do about thirty set-ups a day.

When did your day start today?

Six-thirty or seven in the morning; sometimes [it lasts] fourteen, sometimes sixteen hours.

Do you have any life outside of working on the show?

The nicest thing about a series is, if you're on for more than one year, you have a two-month vacation ... which is very nice. How many businesses let you have two months off?

What's your essential contribution to the show?

Basically, I see my job as deciding what the show's gonna look like. That encompasses where you put the camera, what lens you put on the camera, how high the camera is, whether the camera moves ...

Some directors give you very general guidelines – like they say, "Bring it way in, then we'll have a wide shot over here." Very, very, very few directors will say, "I want a twenty-four millimetre lens, then we'll start here, boom up here, come over here, and then push in a few feet." Very few directors do that; most directors are much more general, especially on a series where you've done nineteen episodes.

So the director says, "Let's bring Roy in through the doors, then go to a group shot," so I'll sort of place the actors to the lens and say, "Back an inch, forward an inch," and I'll pick out the lens size, lay out the dolly track [to move the camera along].

I notice you shoot most scenes with two cameras. Why is that?

You see, we have so many people [in scenes] that, very often, if you can sneak the second camera in and pop off a close-up here and there, I guess there's a rule of thumb that producers have that, I believe, is something like, "If you can get four shots out of the B-camera [the second camera] in the course of a day, it's paid for itself."

You concentrate on the lighting a lot ...

Being a D.P. is all about lighting. How people look tells you how they feel and tells you the story.

You know: tell the story, tell the story, tell the story. How can you tell the story?

You tell the story with how you place the camera and how you light people ... you know, you've got five people in a scene, but whose story is it?

[Say in this particular scene that] it's Roy's story, Captain Bridger; he's the one who's ship's being confronted ...

So how do you stage [that] scene? Let's put him in the foreground. Compose a frame where he's visually the centre of interest. Tell the story ...

You want to direct the audience's attention to the character that, at any given moment, is telling the story. Very often, that means moving the camera. So you lead the audience through the set to the right people at the right time.

And that's not on the script page, is it?

It's *under* the page ...

What you do is you watch rehearsals, and you see how the actors are relating; it gives you a clue [about] how you want to relate them ...

Sometimes [all it takes] is just the right highlight in the deep background; the right little feel in the background, the right detail ...

Do you ever do anything just for your peers?

I do a lot with colours. I'm not sure that the audience would notice the difference between a quarter CTO and a half CTO [i.e. a colour temperature orange gel that is used to shed a glow of illumination on the set] ... You know, they're all warm, but I would hope that D.P.s would notice the difference, between a half CTO and a full CTO ... just like D.P.s would notice the difference between a twenty-one

millimetre and a twenty-nine millimetre [lens]. I don't think the home audience would. They *would* notice a different feel, because when we have a lot of group shots, what we do on the show is use a lot of wide lenses.

We do a lot of scenes with a twenty-one millimetre, with a seventeen-and-a-half millimetre – what it does is you can still get just as tight on a person, but it opens up the set.

These are sets that you want to see a lot of. You don't want to put on a telephoto lens and only see the actor with an out-of-focus background.

THE CAST
Roy Scheider

It's quite simple: without Nathan Hale Bridger, reluctant captain, there would be no state-of-the-futuristic-art submarine called *seaQuest*, and without Roy Scheider bringing that creation to life, there would be no show of the same name.

Scheider, a movie star making his first foray into series TV.

Scheider himself points out, "An old game. I'm just new to this stuff." He seems, though, to be a quick learner – which is just what you have to be to survive the vicious riptides of network TV.

Well, in your opinion, what's the difference between movies and TV?

Everything is done for "TV recognisability", or whatever that expression is. TV? ...

TV-Q.

TV-Q [an advertiser-oriented measure of both recognisability and likeability]. Yeah. Everything is done to attract an audience – for that [individual episode]. There is no overall long-range thinking of how you build a show to get a *sustained* audience. They think week-to-week-to-week-to-week.

If you look at the shows that are successful, what goes into them that finally makes them successful is a plan of *how to get the audience interested in each and every character* – to care for them – how to make sure that all the characters reflect at least one characteristic of everybody in the audience, so you have someone on the show that *you* care about.

I think because we are a very high-tech show, and because we are an adventure, a *scientific* adventure show on [at] eight o'clock, the network sometimes thinks they can throw traditional story-telling out the window. They can't. They *can't*.

If you were advertising that episode – It's obvious to me that you care passionately about the show.

Well, yeah, it's why I signed on.

How would you design that ad?

I would say – the story [entitled "Whale Song"] concerned whales, the preservation of whales: *Will Bridger Resign or Protect His Best Friend*?

The human element, not the destructive element.

You had several substantive meetings with Amblin during the development process.

Yes, I said, "I don't want to be just a square-jawed captain of a submarine, a totally impenetrable guy." You know, a superman. I want my character to be vulnerable; I want him to be unsure of himself; I want him to be eccentric; I want him to be passionate.

I feel I've tapped maybe five per cent of my capability. Now, did you see "Whale Song"?

I taped it.

Now, on that show, written by Patrick Hasburgh [another of the new writer/producers], we've got some *sentiment* between the characters, we have something *at stake*.

And Steven calls up and tells Tony [Thomopolous, president of Amblin Television] and David Burke and everybody, "That's the best show!"

Well, of course, it's the most human show. It's about people!

You have to understand ... all of this high-tech wears off after the sixth week, and if you don't have human beings that you care about, nobody's gonna watch.

I look at the list of movies that you've made, I would think that in the selection of your projects there's an intelligence at work. You don't just say to your agent, "Yes, sir." You pick 'em.

I do pick 'em.

Steven called me and said, "You're gonna go to a meeting in California." And I said, "Whadya talking about? Why do I have to go to California?" He says, "Because I want them, Amblin, to tell you about it, not me." He said, "I'll be there, but I want you to hear what they have to say."

So I came out here and I listened.

They described this adventure programme about inducing a captain back on to the boat that he designed. The inducement is that it's now the greatest scientific floating laboratory that any ... underwater explorer could ever dream of.

And I'm thinking: *Yeah, to create a character like Captain Nemo* – if he's the kind of guy who, when he's not around, is in the lab or out walking on the bottom of the ocean.

I said, "Yeah, you could do a lot with that character, and with a full crew, twenty-five years into the future, that would be *fascinating*. That could be interesting."

Think how [in the future] we handle problems between the sexes, the social problems, the political problems; the fact that

the UEO is like the UN with balls – all of this is great. The world is divided into confederations, and [the mission is] peace-keeping.

And if this is what we are gonna do, why not?... So I signed on.

What we have to offer at eight o'clock is a wonderful show about the ocean ... Other shows have other things. We've got the wonder and exploration of the ocean, and stories that come out of that.

That's why, if the show gets picked up for another season, what they've got planned for next year is all stories that come out.

The submarine will come up, we will go ashore, we will shoot two or three days every week *out in the open*.

In Florida?

Yes, in Florida. We can go to Hot Springs, we can go to Tampa, we can show all of us in the water with manatees and fish. You can build a following for this show. Bridger could be like the American Jacques Cousteau ... and all his crew would be like his sons.

Then you could explore the quirks?

All of them ... Who's pregnant? Who's sleeping with whom? Why are these people aboard the boat? What kind of people does it take to go off for five, six weeks underwater? What happens to them? We haven't even *touched* this stuff.

What do you know about Captain Bridger that the audience hasn't seen?

You've been told *this* much [the distance between a thumb and a forefinger] about Bridger. I know a lot about him:

I know who his parents are. I know how he got through Annapolis. I know how he fell in love with his first wife; I know what happened. I know how he got interested in dolphins. I know what happened to his son. I know what kind of relationship he had with his son, what his son's loss meant to him.

I know all of that, and we haven't seen any of it.

I've talked about it to directors, I've talked about it to the people at Amblin, and I keep waiting.

How do you know all this about him? Is this your construction?

This is my homework. This is what I've done to create a character that I'm playing.

Tell me a little bit about his backstory.

I'll give you a rough idea. I think he came from a lower-middle-class family in the Midwest, and that he probably never saw [the] water till he was about eleven, and when he did it just knocked him out.

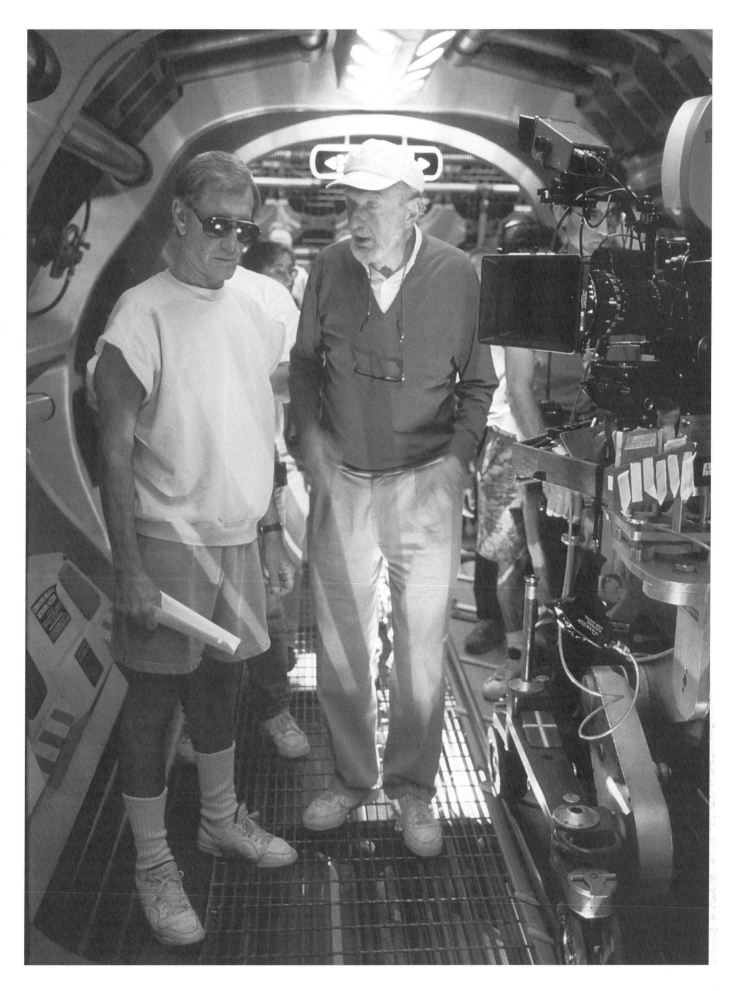

He had a scientist's interest in geology, in biology, in things that grow. He's a great outdoorsman, he loves the outdoors.

His father went to Annapolis, they say in the story, but I don't know about that. I don't know about that. Anyway, he had a very strong and disciplinary father, but his mother – in the backstory, which I like – was a musician, and she is the arts half of the family.

She represents the softer, gentler, more nurturing, feminine side of Bridger, and that enables him to be a scholar, a humanist, a political animal. He's not just in the navy.

Here's a guy who got in the navy because he felt it was the right thing to do, and because he was interested in scientific exploration. And just like [scientist Robert] Ballard, whom this character is modelled after, he knows that in order to do the things he wants to do underwater, he needs the support of the government and the navy to get the money to get the machines to create the submersibles to go down there to do it.

I like the Martian probe episode for that reason.

Yes, yes. The fact that we're in constant competition with people who want to fly out into the universe, and I want to go down [into the ocean].

All those elements are important.

You have to have characters that people care about. That means you have to continue the stories.

Do you have a favourite moment in the show or a favourite episode so far?

Yeah, the one we just did, "Whale Song". And we did one earlier, where the dolphin gets sick and I decide to let the dolphin go back to its pod rather than continuing the mission that I'm on.

Do you know how Captain Bridger met Darwin?

Yes.

How?

He met Darwin because of his wife Carol, who was a marine biologist, and dolphins were her speciality.

It was through observing her in her work that she got him interested in dolphins. Then ... they got married – and I think

his decision to leave the navy during the cold war was a joint decision by both of them – and decided to go off to the islands and just work with the dolphins.

That's what happened. That's when he met Darwin. And Darwin knew Carol. See, we've never tapped that, either. It's so rich, it's so rich. And we haven't done Carol, how she died, what that story was – she got some kind of tropical disease for which there was not enough time to get an antidote, and I had to just watch her die.

How do you find your character? Are you Nathan Bridger when you put on the uniform or when you say the lines?

I'm Nathan Bridger when I get into the situation.

How about rehearsals and setting up and all that?

In television there's no time, no time ... The rehearsal usually consists of just two walk-throughs.

You seem like you're passionate about the show?

[You see] if I put this much energy into it, I want to like it, I want to believe in it ...

If we go to Orlando [to be based at Universal Studios Florida], I want to go down early, sit with all the writers, and *really* discuss the *whole year*, where we're going, what kind of stories we're going to tell, and have some *fun* doing the show.

Stephanie Beacham

Greeting a visitor to her neat-as-a-pin, studio-issue, on-the-lot trailer, she's the picture of poised and wary intelligence. Actress Stephanie Beacham [Doctor Kristen Westphalen] is wearing neatly pressed designer jeans, a white v-neck tee shirt under a pale-blue silk jacket, thick white socks and unmarked running shoes. She's very elegant, very tanned, very L.A. – both prettier and more youthful than on television. Oddly enough, her character was written originally as a man. On the hard, fabric-covered bunk next to her is a cel phone and a bulging black address/phone book – in post-quake Los Angeles, important links to the outside world. Perhaps it's just the British accent and trained diction, but she has a soothing voice just made for reading aloud.

When did you first hear the word *seaQuest*?

I heard about it as definitely *the* hottest new series that was going to be made in 1993. It was definitely the big one. You so seldom get a full season on the air – and this was [an on-air commitment for] a pilot and twenty-two [episodes].

But I hadn't read a script, I'd simply heard about it and asked [my agent] if there was anything for me on it. And the answer was no, there was nothing.

There was a secretary to one of the producers ... and she had worked on *Colbys* in [producer] Doug Cramer's office [there], and knew me very well, and knew that I was nothing like [the character I played] Sable Colby.

She saw people coming and going [auditioning] for Doctor Westphalen, and she said, "That's Stephanie's part." She mentioned me to the producers and they said, "Nope, too expensive and too glamorous."

She said to them, "But I know better," and she told my assistant ... "There's a part for Stephanie. It's going to be a mammoth new series, and it's Stephanie's part but I don't know how to get her in there, because they don't want to know. They have a preconceived idea about what Stephanie is, and I don't know what to do about it."

[My assistant] Janet said, "Oh, Stephanie's just made a new tape of all her work she's done in the last year."

Janet gave one to Elaine [the producer's secretary] and Elaine insisted that Tommy Thompson, who was then the producer, sit down and watch it, and the next day I was in and [the following day] I was cast.

Can you compare this series with other TV you've done?

The situation with a sitcom is the complete halfway house between theatre and television, because you rehearse all week and then you do it live in front of an audience at the end of the week and then it's televised. So that is the meeting place of the media.

I think probably that a *filmed* sitcom is as ideal as you can get, [but] most of them are not filmed, most of them are video. I hate video; I don't like the look of it, and I don't like losing the director from the floor just when you start performing. I like to have the director there in front of me, and the idea that he goes into an electronic box and gives orders to somebody else, who then translates it into technical jargon and just gives it to you, is an alienation that I don't really enjoy.

Westphalen was also someone I was extremely attracted by. My children were sick and tired of me playing baddies, and this was someone far more closer to who I am. She's far more educated [though]; she's got Ph.D.s in genetics, and it's been fun to do the research, to get up to par.

How did you research the character?

Well, the first thing I did was go down to the Scripps Institute and meet ... female marine biologists.

I met a couple of lovely women. One person, Mia Tigner, who *definitely* wasn't the *slightest* bit interested in meeting some Hollywood television actress, [who] suffered fools, you know, not at all gladly.

We were talking for a while and I said, "You're really messy, aren't you?" *"What?"* I said, "You're extremely messy." I mean, wetsuits dripping onto pieces of paper, and she looked at me – and it could've gone either way – and then she said, "Mmm, that's what you think, is it," and she took me into her proper office, and you have never *seen* such a mess! I mean, the

confusion of papers and bits and things! ... She probably knew how to locate everything, but I've never seen such chaos.

But she decided to be amused by my observation, rather than furious, and became a full-blown wonderful human being – which is a bit how I think of Westphalen, in that she's on a sort of another planet – she's not terribly good with people, and quite short with them, but has got a wonderful sense of humour, if her leg is pulled in the correct way.

What do you know about her that I don't know about her?

Just about everything, I think. This is something that I definitely have found fault with in the series, and I think that *finally* the penny has dropped, and what Roy and I have been saying all along is that they won't give a tuppence about these people being in danger, of *any* sort, if they don't know who these people are.

So what I know about her that you don't is that she's been married a couple of times, she's got a daughter, she definitely doesn't regard personal relationships as her most successful area of life.

Why'd you get into the acting game?

I was going to teach movement to deaf people, that's what I *thought* I was going to do, and I went to Paris and I studied mime. I found it very dry.

I was [also for a time] one of the worst au pairs who had ever lived; I was pure negligence, [but] it caused me to be very brilliant when it came to choosing au pairs for my own children, because I knew every trick in the book.

I didn't know what I wanted to do after that, but I had a boyfriend who had just started work at a theatre in Liverpool and I went up there. I hadn't really ever been involved with theatre. I was going to do deaf teaching, because I'm deaf, I'm

very hard of hearing; I have no hearing in my right ear whatsoever. I was born like that.

I just went into this theatre and as soon as I went in I thought, "Ah, this is wonderful, this is wonderful!"

I was the ingenue and the stage manager as well, [but] I was fired from stage management within twenty-four hours for being a distraction. Seventeen and very pretty and I think I talked a lot ... I then went to the Royal Academy afterwards. I did all those things, you know, first witch in the unmentionable play, the Scottish play [i.e. *Macbeth* – speaking the title is considered bad luck by many actors].

I left there [i.e. the Academy] knowing I would only make good French films and good theatre ... then it wasn't French films I made.

I made a few films in Italy, really unmentionable things; I also made some very unmentionable films in England. I mean, the horror films were the only things that were going.

So I turned to television, inevitably; that's what there was to do. It wasn't that I stopped doing theatre.

I can remember sitting at my kitchen table at one point in my life with a play I really wanted to do, a film I really *didn't* want to do and two thousand pounds' worth of bills that had to be paid. And there it was.

I did the film. I called it *Insecticide,* [but] it was called *Inseminoid,* and it is absolutely one of the most ghastly films ever, ever, *ever.* [The play] was a restoration comedy.

What is it about you that the camera really loves? Do you know?

Oh, I love the camera. I think you *have* to love the camera, but I love lighting best. Ken [Zunder, the director of photography] and I have a running thing, because I hate his lighting. I do hate the way submarines have to be lit.

What did you learn from the great actresses you've worked with? You mentioned Ava Gardner.

Oh, she was the first person who ever stood me on a box. I didn't know what she was doing, but of course it was to keep her head up and thus lose the bags under her eyes.

Then Joan Collins of course. Joan Collins was simply wonderful. Just as it was time for my close-up, she'd complain that her high heels were hurting her dreadfully and take her shoes off! Of course, one would just get a nice little box for her to stand on, so it wasn't really a problem. I think you learn more from your own sex than you do from the opposite sex as far as acting is concerned.

Can you think of a trick you've used on this show?

No! I've been able to use none of my really, really most favourite cheap tricks ... Westphalen's complete lack of earrings has nearly got me weeping. Thank God they've allowed me these minuscule pearls now ... They keep saying they're going to, but Roy and I never quite get it together [romantically]. It's

not that one wants to get it together; it's that you want to show it *might* happen. I think a few near misses would be very good.

What would you like to see your character do?

I'd like her to be a full-blown human being with a past and a future. Something that I've never been stuck with before is that you've almost got to take your character back to step one at the beginning of each episode ... That is the one unsatisfactory thing that I find about a television series.

Have you got a favourite moment?

[Long silence.]

There's an episode that's very contentious, because some people liked it and some people didn't, which is called "Games", which is the first episode that we did after the pilot.

There was just a half-second in there where I thought I was all right. I had reason, I had story, I had an audience-understood reason for my actions.

Solving scientific problems fascinates nobody unless they care about you or care about who you're trying to save or care about *something.* Science has to be the background. It's lovely if you can give information, but it's got to be character driven.

It's been difficult to make [Westphalen] as fascinating as I need to make her to want to, uh, um, be there with a hundred per cent, but it's coming. It is happening more now.

My daughters see it [i.e. working on the show] in slightly a camp way. They think it's good news. They're relieved that I'm not dressed in furs, wearing huge rocks in my ears.

Anything that's special about this episode to you?

Yes! I *adore* working with Bob Engels [the new co-executive producer, who not only wrote the episode, but cast himself as mogul Malcolm Lansdowne]; he's just so refreshing as a producer.

What's the quality?

Hmmm, I don't think he'd enjoy it if I said that he was in touch with his female side. I don't think you boys respond very well to that. Roy is [in touch too] ... Roy is available; you can talk to him. There's somebody there ... Roy is lovely; also he's an actor. He's a proper actor.

What would you like to see Westphalen do that she hasn't done yet, apart from the things we've already talked about?

I'm convinced that she just is deeply into some form of homeopathy. I want her to have a huge great fight with big business who make a chemical – what shall we say – a painkiller that is vastly expensive, and she knows that this seaweed would do the same thing. If I'm writing a story for Westphalen, it would be along those lines.

Jonathan Brandis

"Jonathan doesn't need anything from me except moral support," wryly observes his mother Mary, a petite brunette carrying Evian water and dressed in baggy navy sweats and scruffed white walking shoes.

Later she opens the door of his trailer without knocking. "Just a little interview, that's all," says her actor son, and she leaves wordlessly. "Nosy parents," he says with a crooked smile.

Jonathan Brandis, *seaQuest*'s chief teen heartthrob, is refreshingly accessible, unpretentious, and curious. His fellow actors on the show like and respect him and agree that he has what it takes to survive the ranks of Hollywood, which is quickly apparent as he shares an uncommonly serious interest in the mechanics of the business. Contrast this attitude with his trailer; a teenaged boy's bedroom on wheels with one exception – slumped in the middle of the narrow floor is a brown-paper shopping bag, stuffed with fan letters.

Brandis, who turned eighteen in April, is wearing his character's current uniform of baggy tan pants and green shirt. He fills his response with an inordinate supply of ums, ahs and sighs before a fast rush of articulate words. He's clearly savvy about show business and not particularly guarded.

When's the first time you heard the word *seaQuest*?

The first time I heard the title, or heard of the project, was February of 1993. I was up for a couple of other projects at the time – a movie called *Airborne,* a series called *Dudley,* both of which failed, so I'm glad I didn't go with them – and this came along.

And you hear that [Steven] Spielberg is affiliated with it and Roy Scheider – that's gonna draw you to a project. Anyway – and the fact that it was picked up for twenty-two episodes – I auditioned for it, like any other project, and it just evolved from there.

How does the difference between doing movies and doing TV strike you?

I'll tell you. I think it's the closest show, next to maybe *NYPD Blue,* in my opinion that comes as close to feature films as you get. Not because of the content as much as who I'm working with. Roy Scheider and the directors. The pilot was a feature as far as I'm concerned ...

Why did you want to do this show?

It was Spielberg, without a doubt.

Has he given you any advice?

He gave me a bit of advice when we were shooting an episode called "Bad Water" ... on the back lot. He said wear earplugs 'cause you might get an ear infection. That's the only piece of advice.

And I didn't wear earplugs and, sure enough, I got an ear infection.

It's this killing pace on a series. I would think it makes movies look like a piece of cake.

Oh yeah, absolutely. If I was to step into a film right now, it would just be completely different for me.

What was your favourite role before this?

I did a TV movie in 1990 called *It,* Steven King's *It.* It was an ABC mini-series that I was very proud of. I liked it a lot. I mean, I've done films in the past, some of which I wouldn't be doing right now if I got offered them, but they were fun and they were good experiences.

I really feel that this show is a place where I've learned maybe what I want to do in the future and also have learned my craft maybe a little bit better ...

What is it that you want to do now? Do you want to produce, direct?

I'd love to write, produce and direct ... When you learn about the preparation, when you learn how much time it takes, you learn how tough those three are, and I think I've learned that on this show. It's a great grounds for learning anything – editing, anything ...

How'd you get into this game?

My parents got me into it. I hate saying that, because people always take it the wrong way. I don't know if I should tell them that [I'm] *thankful* that they got [me] into it, you know, because of where I am today. You know, they think: "There was *pressure* on him," and all that. It was really a hobby. I did commercials starting when I was four.

What's the first moment you remember as an actor?

The first time I remember being in front of a camera was my first commercial when I was four years old; the first time I remember being an *actor* was when I was about thirteen, fourteen.

I mean, that's when it clicked, that's when kids gain a certain sense about what they're doing and their presence, and how much of an impact they can have on camera ...

You learned your craft the hard way, by making all your mistakes in front of the camera, right?

Yeah, unlike other kids who grew up on a series, which is always tough for a kid. That's why I moved out to L.A. Every one of my friends were on shows at the time and I was the only kid that wasn't on a show. I think that came out to my advantage, 'cause of typecasting and whatever.

Who're your friends? Which shows?

Oh, lots of shows: *Blossom, 90210.* I mean, any show that basically has kids on it; this is a very small town when it comes to kids in the business, and I know mostly every kid that's on television.

Would you be offended if I called you a teen heartthrob?

No, heh-heh-heh, you're not the first –

What's that like? Is it a distraction, is it –

No, no, no. It's, it's good, because it makes you happy.

I'll tell you something: my nephew's life changed with *Sidekicks,* 'cause he now takes Tae Kwan Do and he's become an organised polite little lad. Does that kind of influence bother you?

Things like that don't bother me, that pushes me forward even more. I feel it's terrific if – it's a job, it's work, and you work here every day. This is not fun and games, and the older you get the more you understand the politics of it, the more you understand that it *is* work. And you really don't realise that *people are watching you*, millions of people see this stuff that you're doing ...

Let me ask you some more of the stupider questions: what does that shopping bag full of mail represent?

That represents about half a day's fan mail.

Have you ever gotten fan mail like this before?

Not before the show started. No. David Burke, the executive producer, told me before we started out. He said, "You know there's nothing like a weekly television show and you have no idea how much publicity it's going to generate and how much recognition it's going to provoke," and it's very true ... Yeah, it's a lot.

Do they tell you how many?

Amblin and Universal and NBC say it's like at least three *boxes*, *big* boxes of mail each day.

Do you actually read any of it?

I can't – I read as much as I can; I can't read every single one.

Can you tell me who your typical fan is – girls? boys?

It's interesting: girls write a lot from this show, and *Lady Bugs*; young boys sometimes write from *Sidekicks*, not too often, but sometimes. Girls love to write, so they write constantly.

Is it intelligent stuff, or is it mushy stuff?

A lot of it is very intelligent mushy stuff. That's what it is.

[Laughs]

It's full of admiration for, for the work that I've done, and, and it's ...

[The trailer shakes]

Every time I feel that I think it's going to be an aftershock. It wasn't.

Were you here for the aftershock this morning?

Yes, I was. I was walking to the set.

About the fans –

I think a lot of times they just wanna know what it's like to go to the set each day, and go home with me, and this and that, and know what my life is like. My life really isn't that extraordinary.

I mean, I kinda do my thing, but sometimes they perceive it to be real grand, but it's not, really.

Do you have a problem being in the public eye? Do you feel that you can't do stuff?

What's different about a kid that's on a show and a kid that's in movies versus a kid that's just going to public school, and living what they call a "normal" life, um, is that both those kids go out and, the one kid that goes to the public school that no one knows can jump around and act like an idiot, and no one knows – and no one cares.

The kid that's on the show does that and he's "conceited" and he's "stuck-up" and he's, uh, um, "showing off", and this and that. You're labelled by what you do and how you present yourself.

You also don't get to make mistakes, because you're called on every one.

You *are* able to make mistakes: *on the set* you're able to make mistakes, with family [you're able]; you're not living in a fishbowl.

It's when you go out and do certain events, certain publicity events, that you have to watch what you do and say ... I think that's the case for anybody who has to go somewhere where people are listening to him. It doesn't have to be an actor.

I notice your mom was on the set one day, and then your dad another day. Do they come around all the time?

They do. My dad works during the day, and he stops by in the afternoon. My mom usually comes in and works on the fan mail a little bit.

What do you know about Lucas that I don't know?

I think he appears to be having a good time, but deep down he's making the best out of a bad situation. That's shown little by little on the show. That's something the writers know about, and I know about, that we haven't let on yet to the avid viewers who watch the show a lot. Excluding relationships that he has with the other crew members, he himself is not completely content there. He doesn't fit, he's really a black sheep, I feel.

It goes way beyond sarcasm. That's what it was during the pilot, that's what it was during our original executive producer's reign on the show.

He was, was a sarcastic, bullshitting kid that was rebellious. It goes way deeper than that; now, I understand, it's not about sarcasm. It's not about big words ... he sometimes uses that to justify why he's there. You know, if he runs into somebody who asks him, "Why are you on the submarine?" he might spurt out some computer lingo, not because he has to, but because he has to prove himself, you know? And he's not comfortable completely, but he's happy ...

[Big sigh]

It's not too hidden what he is. I think it's just straight out in the open ... Lucas is probably more intense than I am; I think a little more serious.

What my assumption has been, is that it comes from the abandonment that his father threw upon him when he was younger, compounded by the lack of attention he got from his father, which is something that is definitely going to be continued next season.

Will we meet his parents next season?

I wrote an 18-page treatment [i.e. a short story summary of a proposed plot and characters], on Lucas and his father that I showed to David Kemper, one of our writers, and there's talk of getting together and writing it over hiatus.

That's very smart. Did they ask you to?

No, they didn't ask me to.

What made you decide to do it?

Uh, really nothing. The show had just begun, and if I read it now, it would be completely different, because the show has come so far. It's gone through different executive producers, it's gone through different writers.

What moved you to do it?

I enjoy to write periodically; it's not an everyday thing. Every six months or so, I'll write *something*. It doesn't have to be a treatment for a show ... I enjoy it, but I have to be ready for it ...

Do you remember the first sentence?

[Big sigh]

Do I remember the first sentence? I wrote it back in May [over half a year ago]. It was called "Larency", I remember that; it was about the abduction of ... me [my character]. I can't give away too much because if it turns into an episode I don't want all the little [Questers] to go out and –

Are there Questers?

Oh, I think there are, yeah, I think it's starting to pop up.

Are you going to have your own production company when you get older?

That would be cool ...

How do you find your character?

I think there's different degrees of character in every person you portray. Some characters are very extreme and some characters are not too far off from yourself.

The only thing I have to think about to step into this character is maybe ... he's a little bit younger than he comes across, and at the same time he's much older ... I think that his mind works a lot faster than the average kid. Socially he may be a bit younger ...

Are you computer literate?

No, I'm not. I'm not.

So this is all acting?

Well, no, not all of it, because you have to understand what the heck you're saying.

I think that's a big part of it and I've called on the writers many times ...

I wasn't very comfortable calling up and saying what the heck am I saying? But I've gotten to the point now where it's a necessity. Plus there's *seaQuest* lingo in each script, like MR-3 and MR-4 – those are launches. You start to learn those things ... it becomes like your own vocabulary.

Do you have a favourite moment in the show?

A favourite moment in the show? I have a couple. Yeah. One from an episode called "Brothers and Sisters". It was with

Kelly Martin from *Life Goes On*, and it was a dancing scene that we had in this room.

It was a terrific turning point for the character, because of the fact that it was the first time that he was actually on the submarine, with a girl, a kid his age, away from Bridger.

It was just a little bit of growing up in that one little scene, and it was really special. Really cool. It was written in about five minutes, about five minutes before we shot it, by David Burke, who had just come on the show that day.

Is there something other than in your treatment that you'd like to see Lucas do, or is there something in your treatment?

I'd like to see him, maybe, later on, have a relationship with the other cast members.

I've seen me and Bridger ... I think our relationship has definitely been enhanced since the first couple of episodes ... Me and Stephanie [Beacham], me and Don [Franklin], but maybe not me and Royce [Applegate], me and John D'Aquino more, me and Ted Raimi, and the other characters ...

What're you going to do on hiatus?

Hmm. That's what we're kinda figuring out right now. It's weird, 'cause the chances of finding not only a good project, but a project that's shooting between March and July that has kids in it – it's not very likely. But I'm trying to line up something – a TV movie, anything would be good.

Really? You don't want to kick back?

Hiatus is like summer vacation. When I break for summer vacation from school, I just start to get bored after about three weeks.

When you heard I was coming around to interview you for a book, anything go through your mind that you wanted to make sure to say?

I'll tell you something: I think that this is gonna be *the* hippest show in about twenty-five years.

I think this is gonna come back like *Brady Bunch* did and *Star Trek* did and *Gilligan's Island* did.

It's not a hokey show; I'm not saying that. But it's the kind of show that is timeless. It's like the people in twenty-eighteen are gonna go, "Man! Is that what they thought?! It's great!"

I think that people are really gonna relate to this show in the future, and hopefully they'll learn a lesson from it then, 'cause I think that we're teaching a lot of people now.

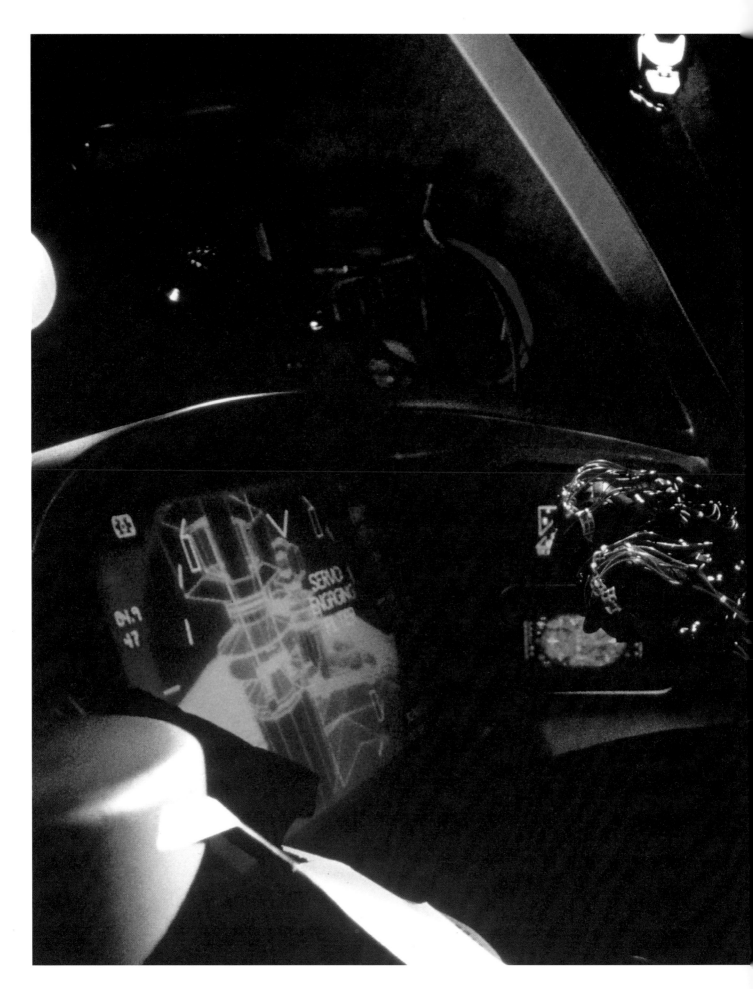

Stacy Haiduk

Get her out from behind those hyper-reality goggles, and you'll find that Stacy Haiduk is one stunning young woman, with a charming smile and an easy laugh.

She's been hanging out all day waiting to be called for her scheduled scenes – shooting the breeze mostly, with her pal Don Franklin – and as night falls, she still hasn't been called, so she figures there's time for an interview and invites a visitor into her small trailer.

She's still in her street clothes, and obligingly she explains, "This is me: unshaven legs with the long dress; it's kind of a long, long peasant dress – scoop-neck collar, buttons all the way down to the ground – mint-green print, flowers, four-leaf clovers. A big black sweater, cashmere of course, and a pair of loafers, black suede." Also, just above one ankle is a kitten tattoo. She giggles. "This is the real me."

Behind her, on the wall, is a framed quotation much beloved by American politicians ["It's not the critic who counts ... The credit belongs to the man who is actually in the arena, whose face is marred with blood, sweat and dust, who strives valiantly."]

It's easily applicable to the struggling actor's life too. Asked impromptu if she can quote it, she does, in its entirety, without once looking, stopping only to ask, "Am I getting it right?"

So why the Theodore Roosevelt quote on the wall?
Brilliant, brilliant, brilliant. Friend of mine actually gave that to me, up in Vancouver, working on a show.

What show?
Round Table.

And why did you need to have this?
'Cause I just think about what he's saying ... It just talks about, Keep going and keep trying and whether you fail and you make mistakes, you have to pick yourself back up and go and do it again, and again, and keep working, harder and harder and harder.

Most people don't do that.

Most people don't get into acting either. Tell me where you were when you first heard the word seaQuest.
I came back from shooting a series called *Route 66.* I had a ball doing that.

I'll bet. Big fun.
Yes, it was. Great people to work with. And my agent said, "We want you to audition for *seaQuest,* and I'd heard about it a little bit – you know, that Spielberg was doing a television series. Didn't know that I was gonna get up on it, and didn't realise

that my agent had sent them a letter, actually a year before, [because] they heard about the project way beforehand.

And I did come in on it, and had fun, did my job, went back, came back again, put me on tape, and I *knew* I did a good job.

I remember looking at the producer, Phil Segal, and I looked at him and nodded my head ... and he nodded back, and I remember walking out and I went up to Big Sur, and they told me ... "They want you."

What were you doing in Big Sur?

[Big sigh]

Relaxing, relaxing.

What did you read at the audition?

Actually they had a scene: I had one scene at the beginning of the pilot, with Captain Bridger. They had me do that scene, which stayed in. And the other scene was with my ex-husband, Krieg, which didn't.

I wish it would've had, because I think it would've given the story between [us] a little more depth.

Tell me what you know about Lieutenant Commander Hitchcock that I don't know?

Let's see. She loves children, *loves* children. She would like to have one of her own one day, but the problem is that she also would like to be the captain of her own ship. So, it's a problem.

In her personal life she would probably love to be married and have all that, but also have the career.

Technically we know a lot about her: she's brilliant. She knows her job. She does it right. She doesn't like taking orders though. That's one thing that's very hard for her. But she does it.

She's very military, but at the same time the frustration of being third in command [means] you sometimes don't [get to] have an opinion. You can't say what you feel may be right.

We don't know about her and Ford; we don't know much about the way she feels about Ford. They're *best* friends, and I think we need to explore more about that: the relationship between them.

Don [Franklin, who plays Commander Jonathan Ford] and I have talked about the relationship.

I mean, maybe at one time, which they'll never show on the show, they did sleep together once, but knew that they couldn't continue that because they worked so close together.

A drunken moment of shore leave?

Yeah, yeah, yeah. It was wonderful once and then –

[Laughs]

I think that adds a little more depth to the characters when we have our scenes together.

What would you like to see your character do that she hasn't done yet?

I'd like to see her open up in an emotional way ... see what her feelings are about ... I would like to see how she feels about being a woman on this ship. Where did she come from? How did she get to be in this position? Where's her family, does she have a family?

What're the answers?

Well, her mother and father are divorced; her father probably lives in Las Vegas, gambling, drunk. Mother ran away with another man. She had a brother that died.

How'd he die?

Drowned, Yeah. Drowned.

Okay. You look like Commander Hitchcock, so how do you become her? Is it when you put on the uniform, say the lines?

Well, I think putting on the uniform is a start.

It starts off with basically going in to hair and make-up. It has a whole different effect on me. Everything becomes a routine, everything is the same. It never changes.

My own personal life changes all the time. Every day is a whole different feeling. But when I come into work, it's the hair, the make-up, I put my uniform on, I walk onto that set, I sit in my chair, and I become Hitchcock.

Is there anything that you say?

I used to. For the first four months of the show I used to meditate, and just get into a place of calmness and a place of mind-setting of where she would be at that point.

Did you have, like, a Hitchcock mantra?

Sort of. Yeah. The music and everything would be very mellow music, very classical music. And I'd just lay down and go through a ritual, if you want to call it, of, ummm, the whole history of her, just very quickly ... and now I don't have to do it that much, because it's become much more simple for me ... to just walk in and do it.

Do you have a favourite moment, something you really liked?

When I sang.

[Laughs]

I had a blast.

Why did you like that so much? I mean, the answer's obvious, but tell me anyway.

I think everyone has that fear inside to sing, but when they get the chance, especially on national television, for the first time in their life, to like, *sing*. A full song. By themselves. And really do it.

Well, I suppose somebody else could've come in to do it. But I wanted it really to be Hitchcock's voice, and what kind of music would she sing. It was fun to find it.

How many takes?

We did three takes.

Does doing this show take over your life? Do you have time for a life?

Well, no. Not really. I'm just starting to have a life, because they haven't worked me as much the last few shows. So I have parts of a life. It's real hard, though, because you get so exhausted you just want to sleep.

What do you do during the hurry-up-and-wait parts of being on TV?

Don Franklin is my buddy, and we will chat and talk about what's going on in the world and what's going on with our lives. I'll read. I just finished reading a book on Marlene Dietrich, which was fascinating.

And I love reading poetry, and I'll just hang in there and write my thoughts down, what I'm feeling.

When you were a child in Grand Rapids, dreaming about *this*, you must have envisioned it – is it anything like you expected it to be?

Nah.

[Laughs]

I thought it was a *little more* glamorous, you know? I saw all those beautiful women in all those gorgeous gowns [in old movies on television], and they got to do these wonderful romantic roles. Kinda how I pictured it: *everything* was romance.

Has it ever been like that?

God, *no*.

Were you on set the other day when everybody went 'It's a nuclear warhead!' during rehearsal?

[Laughs]

Yes, I was the one who started it. "And everybody now! ..."

You organised that?

Yes, I did, because it was just too funny. You know, we're doing a scene, and Captain Bridger says, um, "Well, what is it?" And I don't say anything, and [then] I say, "It's a ... wrecking ball." And I say, "No, no, it's not a wrecking ball." And he says, "What is it?"

And I said, "Everybody now!" And we *all* said: "IT'S A NUCLEAR WARHEAD!"

[Laughs]

It was *sooo* ridiculous.

[Laughs]

Gosh ... It was just one of those moments.

Don Franklin

Don Franklin, settling into a chair in front of a mirror to get powder daubed on his chin, is warbling off-key to a Beatles' tune playing in the make-up trailer outside stage twenty-eight: "Yesterday! All my troubles seemed so far away ... then I got cast on *seaQuest* and ... yooou knnoooow the rest!"

"Very good," someone says sarcastically evoking a hearty laugh out of Franklin. "It sucked."

His brief make-up session over, Franklin heads back to his own nearby trailer, which, with its sprawl of CDs and books and a gym bag spilling with clothes looks "lived in", as he concurs – more so than most of the other sparsely decorated, sterile-feeling mobile homes where the actors spend so much time waiting for their on-set calls.

Perhaps because the young actor is forever being cast as sober and serious, if not downright uptight, straight arrows, it comes as a surprise to discover he has an easy laugh and a wicked sense of humour.

Where were you when you first heard the word seaQuest?
In my dining room, heh-heh.

Tell me about it.
Well, my agent called and said, "We don't know too much yet, they're still in the preliminary stages, *but* over at Universal they're talking with Steven Spielberg's company about doing this show called *seaQuest*."

I said, "Really? What's it about? Is it a futuristic kind of space kinda show?" "No, no, it takes place underwater, blah-blah, blah. Steven Spielberg is executive producer, he's real excited about it."

I thought it sounded *great*. I'd been looking for something for a long time. I'd turned down a couple of things, because they weren't quite right, and this fit right into what I wanted to do ...

Eventually, I went in for a meeting. My first meeting, I didn't read anything. We just talked about the show and the concept, where they wanted to go.

How'd you start out in acting?
I remember in grade school, doing little musicals and such, and then of course I was singing and doing that in high school.

I was also working outside of school, in the local community theatre.

Did your folks push you to get into it?
No. They didn't like it.

You always wanted to do it?
Yeah. But they weren't crazy about it.

What do they think now?
Are you kidding? They're my biggest fans! Hah-hah!

What did you turn down to do seaQuest?
I turned down *The Program*, that football film, and *Walker, Texas Ranger,* another series with Chuck Norris.

As his sidekick?
Exactly ... It's been done before.

After two hour shows to your credit, what made you go back to do another?
In large part, I think it's because of the material. The last thing I was on [*Young Riders*], it was in the old west ... So I go from the eighteen-sixties to the twenty-first century. It's the opportunities that it offers.

Before that you were a Nasty Boy.
Yeah, I played an undercover narc, a cop, in Vegas, and before that I did a show called *Nightwatch* for ABC, where ... I played this leader of this Guardian Angel/Neighbourhood Watch-type group. That was my first ...

How were those earlier acting experiences?
Nightwatch, it was my first show ... and I just wanted to break into the business at that point. It dealt with a lot of really important issues, and also I liked doing something, you know, urban contemporary. It had an edge to it, which was cool.

Then *The Nasty Boys* came along. It kind of afforded me an opportunity to go into a world that I had never been involved in, which is sort of like the underground gang world ... I was sort of the gun expert [Nasty Boy] ... and I was the only one of the cast members who had never held a gun in his life. So they took us to a range in Vegas and started teaching us. It was wild!

And who can turn down a western? ... About a week before we started shooting, they sent me up to a range in Canyon Country [near L.A.] for what they call Cowboy Camp. Heh-heh. And they taught me how to be a cowboy. You know, how to ride, a little bit of roping techniques, how to use a bullwhip, which was sort of my character's trademark. He never carried a gun, he used a whip.

And in this show? What did you have to learn for this one?
Patience. Heh-heh. Yeah, patience. We started the pilot in March, we finished it in August. *Patience.*

It was wild. The show went through so many changes with new writers, new producers. We changed executive producers at one point; it was like a rollercoaster ride – trying to find the show, trying to find the soul, the essence of the show.

Can you tell me what it is?

I think we're still finding it.

I think it's a lot of things, but I think we're still finding it.

It's a big cast, there're a lot of people, which I think is an asset. Some people see it as a deficit, but I think it's an asset to have all those different personalities on the show.

And of course the special effects. That's all fun. It's kinda fun to be able to go on stage and not really have to fake a whole lot: you push a button on screen and what you need is *there*.

There's very little blue screen or green screen.

It's kinda neat ...

I dug *Star Trek* when I was a kid.

In this last episode, you had William Shatner guest-starring. How was it working with Captain Kirk?

Captain Kirk ... Hah! That's just it, it was kinda hard not to see him as anything but.

Captain Kirk! He'd be doing a scene totally serious, and I'd be just quaking inside – Hah-hah-hah: *My God, Jim! It's a dolphin! A talking dolphin!*

That last episode was the earthquake episode, during the shooting the earthquake hit. Did that affect you?

Oh yeah!

It was scary ... It was just so violent! ...

There's talk about moving the show to Florida. I can't wait!

I don't particularly even like living in Los Angeles to begin with. I wouldn't want to raise my kids here.

Do you have kids?

No, not yet. But we're in rehearsals now.

Let me ask you a couple of *seaQuest* questions: What do you know about Commander Ford that I don't know?

Hm. Well, I don't know if you know it or not – it depends on how much you've watched the show and how perceptive you are as an individual ... how anal-retentive he is. *Hah!*

He is that.

Yeah. If you ever go into his room, and I hope that we will next season ... *everything* is perfect ...

What would you like to see your character do next season that he hasn't done before?

I'd like to see them explore his anal-retentiveness. I'd like to see people make an effort to loosen him up. I'd like to see *him* make an effort to loosen up, and I'd like to explore how he does that:

What kind of music does he listen to? Does he like to dance, does he ever go out dancing? Why doesn't he have a girlfriend? What about the girls back home? Who does he call when he calls home? Those kinds of things I'd like to explore, as well as my relationships on the ship.

Now, the only one who's really an old friend of mine on the ship is Hitchcock [played by Stacy Haiduk], and that's something that really hasn't been dealt with.

Hitchcock's been through a bad marriage, and I'm sure I know *all* about that ...

Do you know the answers to all those questions?

Yeah, I do.

Has Ford been married?

No, he's never been married. He went through a phase when he was in college where he was dating *a lot*, and it was getting him in trouble, it was distracting him from what was important.

Eventually, being the anal-retentive, all-or-nothing guy that he is, he just sort of said, *"No More!"* and focused on his career, which is why he got to the point where he is.

Did what happened in the pilot episode really make him nuts? He had to pretend to be incompetent to get Bridger to take command.

Yeah. I think that was really, really hard for him. He had to deal with *that* – other people's perception of him – and to do what he was ordered to do. He's a soldier ...

How do you find the character?

That's a good question, because I have been endeavouring to find this character for a long time, and as the series has gone on, as they've written more episodes and explored more, I discover more, because a lot of my questions are what-ifs. That's how I like to approach a character, as opposed to having a few things that are in concrete.

Could you give me an example of that?

Yeah. For instance ... "Bad Water". In the middle of a hurricane in that show, *What if* Ford is stranded and he's responsible for these four people. *He's* scared and people are being flip. Krieg [played by John D'Aquino] is being flip. He's got to figure out what to do, but he's afraid that he's going to die at the same time. How does he handle that? Well, Ford gets real brittle in situations, he loses his sense of humour ... That was one what-if that occurred to me. He's underwater in the one we're going next week [the episode entitled "Abalon"] ... He's deeper than any man's ever been, in this suit, six *miles* under water ... Alone.

Oh, you get to meet the mermaid?

Yeah, I get to meet the mermaid. *What if* I'm down there, and *what if* I'm in danger of nitrogen narcosis or that sort of thing? *What if* I am hallucinating? *What if* I am incompetent? Those kind of questions drive Ford ... It's gonna be real interesting for me to explore that. I will sort of "paint the borders" on the scene myself, and I'll add the primary colours that I want, but once I'm in the situation that's when I sort of improvise, sort of *paint* and let it go, let my instincts go. That's where the fun of creativity is for me.

Is this a more difficult character for you than the *Young Riders* character and the *Nasty Boys* character?

You know, I think it is, and the reason is because, for a long time I didn't think I was right for this role.

This is the first role I've done in a long time where I really didn't think I was right.

What did you think was the problem?

I think when I read the script and everything – Commander Ford – I kinda thought of this sort of, ah, big Avery Brooks-type character, with this James Earl Jones voice and these linebacker shoulders and granite chin kind of deal.

Then I met Bob Ballard, and Bob Ballard *is* a captain, Bob Ballard runs ships; he's not only a scientist, but he *is* a captain. And this is a soft-spoken man, who's very intelligent, who is very iron-willed, and I thought:

This is a human being; Ford is a human being. He can be soft-spoken at times; he can be commanding at times; he can be a myriad of things that perhaps didn't fit in to my initial stereotype of what I thought a commander would or should be. So that gave me a lot more confidence in going forward.

Royce D. Applegate

Musician, radio D.J., stand-up comic, film and TV writer. Actor.

A man with a familiar face, he could just as soon be a face you remember from high school as he is that guy in that Kim Basinger movie – whatever role he's playing you can count on him to deliver a solid, nuanced performance, as in his brief turn in the remake of *The Getaway*, and as he does every week as Chief Manilow Crocker on *seaQuest DSV*.

Despite having the credit of co-author of *Loose Shoes*, a ribald sketch comedy that was Bill Murray's first movie, Applegate is a serious-minded, thoughtful craftsman. It's a blue-collar stance that easily commands respect among his peers.

What kinda writing did you do?

I'd written for the old TV show *Welcome Back, Kotter*. The last year it was on, I was on staff with them. And then there was a spin-off from that called *Horshack*. There was a pilot and three episodes that never made it on the air. I've had a couple of low-budget screenplays produced.

You always wanted to be an actor?

I did. I was one of those kids ... from a real early age it was what I wanted to do. It took me a long time to do it – not in the sense of like school. I did a lot of dramatics in school, and was voted best actor in junior high school. But then I went away to the University of Oklahoma, and it was time to get a real job and study something for real.

How'd you get to be a writer?

Actually, while I was still in Dallas. I'd left the pharmaceutical firm and I'd taken a job to get as close to show business as I could in Dallas, with a radio station there.

I was married and had a kid at the time – trying to get out to the movie industry. Since I couldn't get out there and represent myself, [I tried] writing a screenplay, which I could send out ...

You sent it out cold?

I made fifty copies of it and sent it out cold, and I got some reaction to it.

Was *Loose Shoes* the old joke that got what's his name into so much trouble?

Yes, it was. It was originally called *Coming Attractions*... coming attractions for non-existent movies.

The loose shoes one was an all-black, sepia-toned forties musical number ... It looks like one of those great old thirties, forties things.

We had an all-black orchestra and they would stand up and do their horns together ... and on the drums it said The Earl Butz Band. That was supposedly who first told the joke.

Back up a second: you're in Texas, you send out a spec script – how did you get from there to Bill Murray?

This was after I got out here. I worked with The Committee, an improvisational group out here ...

So you followed the spec script to L.A.?

What happened was, I'd gotten some interest from agents when I sent it out. That told me, well, maybe I can write. I wasn't sure.

I even had to look in the library for what form a screenplay was supposed to be done in ... [But before that, there was a club in Dallas where] I started doing a stand-up comedy act. Somebody from the Playboy Club saw and I got on their circuit. That was what ultimately brought me to L.A.

That got me out here and I started working with The Committee improv group. Casting people would come see. My first acting job was *That Girl* ...

This is the first series?

I've had four or five failed pilots ... I've been a semi-regular on *Houston Knights* and on *Flamingo Road*, but this is the first full-time series.

How does the writing help the acting and vice versa?

How the writing helps is when I get scripts – just dialogue-wise or scenic-wise, you learn structure in writing, also dialogue – a lot of the scripts I get I find that's not always there.

So when I started being an actor, when I'd go in for interviews – I didn't know any better – so I would sort of not *change* the lines but would sort of personalise them, and often give a little twist on the ending. Or after I'd get the job I'd do the same thing.

What I said in my head was, I'm gonna make them tell me, "Don't do that." I knew better than to just go in and say, "Can I do this?" 'cause they'd just say, "*No!*" So in rehearsal I'd always throw it in and they'd say, "Keep it! Keep it! That's great, keep that!" So I think it's helped me in that way.

I believe an actor is hired to contribute, more than just recite the lines – not to write the script, but to bring some humanity or personality to it or something.

Can you cite an example from *seaQuest*?

Oh gosh, no. I can cite one recently 'cause I did *Gettysberg*. I had a real nice role as a Southern general, General Kemper.

I did some research on my character and found a couple of things that happened that were just great scenes. He was shot off his horse, and in the screenplay that was the last you saw of him, except General Lee asks, "What's the status?" And [the reply is], "This general, this general and this general, and General Kemper is down and thought to have been captured."

And I found in the Civil War books, he was shot from his horse and Northern troops grabbed his body and were carrying it toward their lines, and his own troops rushed forward and grabbed his body and brought it back.

He was still alive?

He was still alive, but he was an invalid. But he thinks he's gonna die. He was actually carried on a stretcher to the rear ranks after the battle was over and he passed General Lee, and General Lee – this was what I found in the books – said, "Who is that general?"

And they said, "General Kemper," and he said, "I must speak to him," and there's this wonderful scene.

So I went to the director and said, "Look, there's this great scene that actually happened." He said, "Write it up, we'll do it."

So I wrote up the thing with the Northern troops grabbing his body, and they shot that, and the scene with Lee at the end, and it becomes this great scene on the screen, because it's like you think he's gonna die. They had Lee looking out over all the troops, going "It's my fault, it's all my fault," and in the books that I found it was when they brought Kemper's body by [that] they had this dialogue:

Lee says, "I hope you're not too seriously wounded," and Kemper says, "They tell me that it's mortal, General," and he says, "I hope that's not the case. Is there anything that I can do for ya?"

And Kemper says, "There's nothing you can do for me, but see to it that full justice is done my men who have made this charge today," and Lee says, "I will" and salutes and he's

carried off. And they put that in and it's one of the better touching scenes.

Do you remember the first time you heard the word *seaQuest*?

It was when I went on the reading. This job has been one of those amazing ones because it happened so easy for me and so quickly. I almost didn't have time to get worried about it or anything.

Usually, you go in, you read, if you get in the finals they put you on tape, then they take you in to meet the network, and usually they have two other people, or three other people for the same role.

On *seaQuest,* I went in, read, met [the director of the pilot] while I was there; after I'd read the first time, they put me on videotape immediately, that day, and I still hadn't heard much about the series.

I knew it was Amblin, I knew it was Spielberg, so that was a big deal. I really liked [the character] – I was once in the marine corps, so I knew this character – he was the old master sergeant.

So, three weeks later, I went in to read for the network, and I was the only one that they brought in for the role. So it was sort of my job to lose, rather than my job to win.

What can you tell me about Crocker that I don't know?

To me, when I saw the breakdown on the characters and everything, he's the guy I knew in the marine corps, who's been in for twenty-five years.

He probably should've been an officer a long time ago, but he's the kind of guy who was a little wild and rebellious, mouthed-off a lot to authority and what have you, but he knows everything. He's a real good soldier.

And now it's twenty-five years [later], he's calmer, but he knows as much as any of the officers in terms of how, you know, to run things, and he's sort of like a shop foreman in an auto factory or something like that.

He's the guy, if you want the thing to work right, he's the place you go, but they keep hiring new young vice presidents out of college; they're not going to bring him in off of the floor. So he has a power base, particularly as security chief, that allows him to arrest an officer if he feels the need to, but he's the ultimate good soldier, and he and Bridger were friends years ago, in the old navy of ninety-four, so Bridger knows him and trusts him and the younger guys respect his knowledge and his time in.

What would you like to see him do that he hasn't done?

I'd like for them to delve, or at least let us get to know more about who he was, which tells us who he is.

In my own head I had to invent a little life history for him, because there never was one. I saw him as a guy who was married to the navy but he's been married three times. All of his ex-wives love him; he's got, you know, nine kids out there, but they all understand that he's married to the navy, basically, that they were secondary to the navy.

As security chief, he once was the young rebellious sailor, so they can't run any numbers on him, because he's run all the numbers himself before he became security chief. He's been locked up by the shore patrol a couple of times.

You know, I was telling 'em, "I play a little guitar, it'd be neat if you just had a little thing where you walk by his quarters and he's sitting in there playing guitar." It'd tell us something about him.

Do you have a favourite moment or episode?

Oh yeah, the episode "Bad Water", which David Kemper wrote, was really a wonderful episode for Crocker.

It was the one where they're stuck in the life raft with the hurricane ... and most of the officers are up there, and we get hit by lightning. It's the one where I sing the whaling song.

Everybody gets really nervous and the young guys are real anxious, and I look around and see that and just get 'em all fired up singing this song.

Then also I had that nice moment with Roy, where he's really down, because he trailed out the antenna and we got struck by lightning. I go to him and say, "Permission to speak freely" and "It's not your fault," that sort of thing.

That's what I think [Crocker] can do. His value is that it's the one place that the Bridger character can go and get an honest opinion that's not coloured by his bars. They're old friends and Crocker, he knows, will shoot it to him straight, even if they don't agree. Crocker will give him his honest opinion.

Do you ever find the pace of series work to be brutal?

It is ... I've made a living as an actor for twenty years, worked all the time – it's all been guest stars, sort of bad guy or good guy of the week – and I used to watch people who are series regulars on *The Tonight Show* or something like that, and they would be sort of bitching and moaning, and I'd be going, "Oh, you cry babies!" But once I got on [the show], it was like, "Oh, okay, I understand now."

The first month or month and a half, I was trying to fit the series into my life, and finally I just had one of those revelations – *Oh I'm doing this wrong, I'm gonna have to fit my life into the series!* ...

[But for] the kid in me who always wanted to be an actor, this is the perfect pay-off, because I like science fiction, it's a great role ... I [also] strap on a gunbelt every day and tie a holster to my leg.

About five or six shows in, I was strapping it on one morning, and I went, "Gee, I'm the town sheriff too! In addition to everything else, I'm the town sheriff."

Ted Raimi

Ted Raimi seems an easy-going guy, candid and enthusiastic. With a long narrow face, a high forehead, and prominent ears, Raimi draws you in with his frequent flapping hand gestures.

A visitor often spots him in his blue *seaQuest* uniform, hanging out on the soundstage between on-set "calls", perhaps in intense conversation with a grip, gloriously recounting his Arizona weekend to do a few scenes as an Old West accountant in his brother's latest movie, or chatting up a pretty extra, his eyes glinting behind thirties-style wire rims. His Dutch grandfather emigrated to Detroit in 1905, and that's where Ted and his older brother, film director Sam Raimi, were raised. He went to N.Y.U., Michigan State and the University of Detroit, minoring in English and majoring in acting at all three. Ted followed his brother to Southern California – not, he says, to break into show business, but for the free rent.

When did you first hear the word *seaQuest*?
December of ninety-three.

So you were hired pretty early on?
Yes, I was.

Was anybody else cast at that point?
I think Roy Scheider probably was.

Tell me the circumstances.
It happened very much like many auditions happen. I was at a point in my career before I got the show where I was not doing very well acting-wise.

Really?
Yeah, you go through peaks and valleys ... and it happened to be a valley. The Grand Canyon at that point, I think.

I was striking out a lot and I went in to read for *seaQuest*. I read the script and thought it was great. It's one of these shows, you know, where enthusiasm counts – it counts in this business like in any other business – and I was really enthused and inspired by the show, because I'd always been a very big science fiction fan, and here was some science fiction I *really* liked.

It was the kind I had read as a kid in my old back issues of *Amazing Stories* and *Amazing Tales*, but the real ones [the comic books] not the TV show. These are the ones I'd collected from garage sales and had fifties original Richard Matheson in them, you know? You a *Star Trek* fan?

Yeah, I'm a science fiction fan.
Okay, so you know what episode he wrote, Matheson? ... Matheson wrote "Mirror, Mirror", where Kirk is split into two

personalities. Anyway, these are magazines that I would covet as a kid, and, uh, I used to get made fun of a lot when I was a kid, and these were a way out.

Why? Were you like a ninety-eight-pound weakling kid or what?

Kind of, yeah. I was very awkward, had braces until I was like fourteen or fifteen ... I did not excel in sports at all ...

So when did you get into acting?

In high school.

As a way to get the girl?

No. I wasn't interested in that. I really just wanted some friends. Acting was something I could do; it was a club I could join at school ... Here was a way to explore all these fantasy elements [like science fiction] in a real way ... In fact, that is what I still find most appealing about the business ... So, anyway, I joined acting as a kid in high school and suddenly I had some friends, which I'd never had before.

So when did you come west?

Right after I went to the University of Detroit. I came out to California because I have a brother who's a filmmaker, who you may or may not know.

I don't know him personally, but I know his work.

He had a place out here. The truth is, I wish I could tell you I came out here for a burning desire [to act], but it was free rent and I had just finished up at school, so I said, "Hey, Sam, I'm kinda moving in with ya."

How much older is he than you?

Six years.

And he was already established then?

Yeah, he was established somewhat. He's made two movies by then. One was a success – *Evil Dead* – and the other one had been a failure for him ... [Later] my brother also directed *Darkman*.

And you were in it?

I play Rick ... a very bad guy in a slick gang ...

Sam had a very good idea for that one. He said, "Why don't you play it a little gay? So you and Larry [Drake, who played the bad-guy leader of the gang] can sort of be lovers in this."

There were a lot of protests ... I said, "Look, I'm not a gay gangster, I'm playing a gangster who happens to be gay." I was

just making an interesting acting choice, I wasn't trying to upset anybody.

It was at that point that I realised how powerful what you do on screen is translated to people. It's amazing. And this show especially.

I've never done TV before. Now I find as I watch and talk to people who view the show on a weekly basis how – they're not stupid people, but they get confused because they see you every week.

They think they know who you are, and you do something strange on the show and you get a million letters.

Let me ask you about William Shatner, given that you're a *Star Trek* freak.

Yeah, it was a thrill. I mean it was nice to know, to see that he's actually a very good actor. I had thought, watching his stuff as a kid, that he was great, and as I got older, I went, "Well, maybe it was just 'cause I was a kid, a *Star Trek* fan, but ... he's really very talented.

He's very intense.

Yes, he is, and he knows his stuff.

I did a little research on him and I found out he's done a lot of Broadway. He'd actually been in the original *Shot in the Dark* [on Broadway] ... He was the original Inspector Clouseau.

Working with him on the bridge, I kept getting confused, 'cause I'd look over and there'd be William Shatner giving me an order and for a *second,* for a split second, I'd think I was on the *Star Trek* set.

What was the earthquake like around here? That was the episode you had to take four days off.

Actually, we went back to work pretty quick. Most of California didn't. Movies are funny that way, you know. They're not human. There's everything else and then there's movies. That's the way the film business looks at itself. It's very odd. And the earthquake was a very good example of that, you know.

Everybody stayed off work until Monday, but we are the movie industry. IBM thcy close their offices till Monday. Schools were closed for weeks, [so] kids don't learn. But this is Hollywood, we put movies out.

Which is fine ... I think the roads were perfectly safe the next day, except for the ones that were closed. I had no problem going back to work.

What do you know about your character that I don't know?

Well ... this is all actor stuff, so it might sound strange: O'Neill grew up in a very sheltered family in northern Michigan, wealthy family, and he was sent to all these very expensive East Coast schools, majored in languages.

Being that age, he was very rebellious, so he decided to take a career when he graduated from college that was as far away from that kind of life as he knew. So he joined the military. And so, that's how we know the O'Neill of today.

I think he's a very smart guy, very well educated, but he also has kind of an anger and kind of a rebellious side as well.

Where does that come from?

Just oppressive parents, I think. That's the life I gave him anyway.

What would you like to see him do that he hasn't done yet?

Well, O'Neill, I made him so shy and reclusive that I think it would be interesting to see him really go ... *berserk* one episode.

It would be interesting if we could develop him, because you know Ford and Bridger and most of the other people are very aggressive characters. I've intentionally made mine a little shy and closed, just so it would be a little more unusual. That's how he's written, too.

I'd like to see him maybe throw some punches, maybe get into some trouble. It would be very interesting to see how he could handle that.

Do you have a favourite moment or episode?

There's a moment in "Bad Water" where Ford and his party are trapped on the surface, and I can hear his Morse code from the camera auto-wind he's sending out. Everyone's cheering for Ford, everyone's [excited] that we [found them],

and I'm telling everyone to be quiet because all my pals are up there. They're dying.

I stand up and tell everyone to shut up.

That's a great moment. It's very human and it's very unlike O'Neill. I think that it gets down to the core, he's respectful of order up to a point. And then, to do the right thing, he will go berserk. I'd like to see more of that.

Do you tell the producers these things?

No, not really. When we talk sometimes, I say I think it might be a good idea to do this or that, but not really. I leave the writing up to the writers and I listen to what they have to say.

How do you find the character?

It's really all about uniform. I put the uniform on and my glasses and I'm O'Neill.

Those aren't your glasses?

They are my glasses, but the glasses with the costume are another thing.

What are you going to do on hiatus?

I'm going to make a movie.

A done deal?

Nope, but it's called *Dirk Sliprock Swings*. It's a comedy that I wrote.

Tell me about it.

It's about a nebbishy composer who falls in love with a beautiful singer, and to impress her he completely changes his personality to this hip, swinging jazz cat.

He learns to play jazz music and he becomes Dirk Sliprock by night and her friend, Roderick Slipstein, by day.

When did you write this?

I came up with the idea a long time ago, when I was in high school. As I told you, I used to get picked on a lot. Who doesn't think: wouldn't it be cool, really, to be one of those guys? They get all the girls, they're slick, they always know what to say, they're always right on the money ...

Where'd the name come from?

A character I saw once on *The Three Stooges*: a crook names Slip – "Hey, it's Slip. He's gettin' away."

And I just thought Rock was always good, like Rock Hudson. I used to do my own character. I'd say [unctuous, narcissistic voice]: "Hey, girls, I'm Dirk Sliprock," and I'd get a lot of laughs.

John D'Aquino

John D'Aquino is on a killer schedule: daytimes, he's on the *seaQuest* sets, playing wisecracking Lieutenant Benjamin Krieg, a part that was created with him in mind by his friend Tommy Thompson, the series' former executive producer; nights, he's treading the boards as the leading man in *Caribbean Romance*, a romantic comedy being mounted at a local theatre.

But despite the pace, he seems downright serene, happy to be acting, living his childhood dream. With a start in the business that puts Lana Turner to shame, D'Aquino recounts how he was discovered while tending bar – not by a William Morris agent, but by the chairman himself. As he tells it, three months after this exchange, he was on his first series:

Customer: "Are you an actor?"

John: "The busboys are actors, the waiters are actors. Everybody's an actor here. The chef is an actor. Diet coke?"

Customer [actually the William Morris chairman, who's about to offer his business card]: "Are you any good?"

John: "Yeah, I'm good. Shrimp cocktail?"

Now, a decade later, D'Aquino's most obvious concern is to explain – from the outset – to a *seaQuest* outsider the fine line he feels obliged to maintain:

He's careful to be professionally proper and loyal to the new regime that supplanted the friend responsible for him being on the show, while remaining personally loyal and proud of his old buddy, with whom he first made the aspiring actor's obligatory pilgrimage to Hollywood.

Politics are a part of any show – probably part of any high-stakes endeavour that involves many scores of participants with diverse, and sometimes diverging, interests. Still, it's an unenviable position to be in; particularly for anyone who's ever navigated the sharp shoals of behind-the-scenes Hollywood.

Tell me the first time you heard the word *seaQuest*?

I was in Tommy Thompson's office. I was co-writing a *Quantum Leap* at the time, [an episode] called "The Beast Within". I was actually writing it and Tommy was helping me. He was one of the producer's over there. I think he told me that he'd gotten a telephone call ... they were interested in him taking over the helm at *seaQuest*. This must've been December of ninety-two ...

Tommy and I drove out to California together from South Florida, giving each other California names: he became Buster and I was Moon Doggy ...

Tommy and I were part of the Burt Reynolds programme in Jupiter, Florida [where the actor has his theatre] ... [Tommy's] like a brother to me ...

Anyway, we set off for California. We've known each other since then, [and] helped each other through a lot ... [Once he'd taken the *seaQuest* position and created the Krieg role] it became the most difficult audition process of my life, because of the personal and the political factors ... behind the scenes. It was more than just John D'Aquino; I became Tommy's guy – and that was either looked at in a favourable or not a favourable light. It became my own character dilemma ...

There was a war going on [at the network] behind the scenes [during the audition process]. A really bad, ugly one.

How'd you find out you got the part?

[Back on the *Quantum Leap* set after the final audition] I heard Tommy was on the set looking for me ...

He told me, and in front of Scott Bakula and a few others ... and we just sat there hugging each other ... you know, at that time our dream came true of working together when we were just kids driving out here together.

Well, let me ask you: is the war over?

I think it is. I have to hope –

When did it end? Did it end last December, when the new regime came in?

I wish I could say it did.

The war might've ended, but the constant proving ground for me continued, because then, after Tommy left, [new executive producer] David Burke came in, certainly an accomplished man with his own ideas ... When a new regime comes in, the old regime – all the problems are laid on them.

Of course.

And I was seeing both sides of it, and I'm not saying that any one particular party was any more right than another, but I literally went to David Burke twice to say, "You know, I'm really tired of being the pawn in the game."

One would hope that it's about the work. In other words, if my work is up to snuff, then you keep me; if it isn't, then you get rid of me ... So all I wanted from anybody was a fair shot, to be able to show my best work ...

When David [Burke] came in, he probably wasn't sure if he could trust *me*. You know, am I a fly on the wall?

Did he think you were going to run back and tell Tommy?

I didn't know ... I wanted to stay out of it. I knew Tommy Thompson and Roy Scheider were having trouble early on, and I told Tommy, "I gotta be clear of this one. You guys can do whatever you gotta do."

I walked up to Roy my first day and said, "Mister Scheider, can I speak to you? ... If you haven't heard already, you probably will that Tommy and I are very close friends ... I just wanted you to know ... that I'm quite honoured to be working with you and I consider myself one of your soldiers here, and I will never compromise you to Tommy. I will never betray any confidence that we have on the set, and Tommy doesn't expect me to, and I wouldn't anyway."

Are you okay with the new administration?

Yeah, I am. I am very much ...

Let's talk about the character some.

That's evolved quite a bit ...

What do you know about Krieg that I as a viewer don't know?

That's probably [the same as] asking, "What do you know about John D'Aquino that I don't know?"

Let's step back then: how do you find the character? What's the difference between Krieg and you?

Well, it's very interesting, because I was pulled aside by David Burke at one point; in a very kind moment he said to me, "You're testing negative at NBC," and he was doing this for my own good 'cause he wanted to say to me, "If ever you see an opportunity to go for the heart moment, as opposed to the top level of the character, find it."

But the other side of that frustration was, the scenes that were being written at that time – and I'm not saying they were wrong, I'm just saying that was the thought at that time – were meant to go for something else. And I was being true to the word, all the way ...

So what do you do to become Krieg? Do you put on the uniform to become him or is it something else?

People on the street ... say to me, in their own definition of Krieg, "He's kind of a slimeball, isn't he? He's kind of a sleaze?"

I think early on that might've been true; I was supposed to be the con man, you know, who really didn't want to be there ... That's the top level of any definition of a supply officer ...

How far could I play that? That's going to get boring for me and boring for the people at home to watch. So what I want to see is the complexity of any human being – just like I don't want to see Ortiz and O'Neill be only military, week-to-week. Otherwise, how long could I listen to that technical jargon? ...

So, tell me what you know about your character that I don't know?

Well, I know he's got a love for life.

I know he'd love to travel the world. I know he'd love to travel the world from above the ocean. I know he's dying to get off that boat. I know he's somewhat claustrophobic ...

I think David Burke is aware of this, as are a lot of the writers: Krieg only does something to the point where he realises that it may be detrimental to someone else ... He's never really out to harm anybody. He just is trying to get ahead.

I also think he's got a great amount of regret over the fact that he wasn't able to become the officer that he set out to be. I think he would've liked to become Bridger, in a way.

Do you know how he got stuck on that boat, given that he doesn't want to be there?

I think initially ... and it was never explained – but initially it was punishment. It was my penance. I was found with the general's daughter.

And my idea of the navy was running operations Club Med-style from above the water, and my penance was to go twenty thousand leagues under the sea for as long as they could keep me down there ...

I would like to explore, *Get me off this boat* ...

What else would you like to see him do that he hasn't done?

I want to see him grow. I don't want to see him lose any of the mischief. I want to see his faults.

David likes that I wear glasses, and that's a coming-to-terms thing with Krieg ...

Do you have a favourite moment on the show? A favourite scene, a favourite episode?

Which wasn't cut?

Or that was cut ... Was your best moment cut?

The one that comes to mind ... it wouldn't have taken much more to let it play out, but when we were on the raft, being blown around by the hurricane –

"Bad Water"?

Yeah. Stephanie's character [Doctor Westphalen] and my character sort of come to terms to some degree – we just basically didn't like each other up until that point ...

We did a moment where we finally became friends. To me, the point is: you only knew that by the smiles on our faces, the way we behaved towards each other *after* the lines were over – there's a tendency to cut right after the words are over – but it was that recognition point – we even hugged right after that – and it was cut.

How much was cut? The speech was left in?

Yeah, it's literally a second or two. It's almost like the point where Don Franklin [i.e. Commander Ford] and I are in that water tunnel ... lock arms, and I'm getting blown away –

When the boat was taken over?

Yeah, the commando episode ... The point of the whole episode, at least from *my* story arc, was that Don thinks truly that I'm out for myself, and that doesn't make an officer. I've got to be out for the good of all the people on the vessel.

So when we get taken over, he sees me responding as an officer should. And in that one scene, Krieg basically forfeits his own life by opening up the water channel. When he and I lock arms ... I said to Don, "You know more about how to save the others than I do. You know the ship. So let me take the fall here"...

You're not going to say a lot when water is rushing [at you] ... but the point of recognition is, where he and I look at each other, eyeball to eyeball, and it's just like, we're two men at this point.

The thing was, I let go. I just let go of his arm, because I know he's got to take care of them. Instead of the water carrying me away, it's Krieg's decision to let go and sacrifice himself.

That's a big story point that was either cut out in editing or we just weren't able to bring it to the film properly.

Does the beginning conflict pay off in the end? He's not gonna recommend Krieg for something?

I guess so.

In the scene with Stephanie, you have the dialogue but you don't have the reaction shot?

Because the dialogue can mean one thing, and the reaction can mean the truth, and the reaction shot was gone ...

Don and I were both upset [about the water tunnel scene] ... that thing we worked so hard for, until four-thirty in the morning, drenched, freezing ... But we [found out we] couldn't do it because of matching the water levels [in the various takes]. It's disappointing, because that's what we worked the whole night to get ...

You said the part was written for you originally: what was there originally that was you?

That's Tommy's perception of me. I think that Tommy perceives that I get things rather easily ...

I just don't talk about all the ones that got away. I try not to focus on that part ...

He knows that I'm a mischievous sort of person, he knows that I like to cut up. He was playing to that ...

This is very important: Tommy's one of the most naturally funny people that I've met in my life. He's funnier than I am, by far. But he knew that I could deliver his rhythm, because he and I were indigenous to the same area, and he knows that I know him.

And that's very important, because as a writer you're going to feel more comfortable if you know that you can turn it over and know that at least the essence of what you intended is going to remain. Eventually [that] becomes a marriage of the actor and the writer's words: the character.

Marco Sanchez

Marco Sanchez, decked out in a black *seaQuest*-brand wetsuit, is sitting in the open doorway of his on-the-lot mobile home, hunched over a book [Professor Stephen Hawking's cosmological best-seller], waiting for his call.

Is there really such a thing as a *seaQuest*-brand that predates the series, a sceptical visitor wants to know.

"See, here's the name right here," the twenty-four-year-old actor with the shy smile and the sincere manner says, pointing to the company logo emblazoned down one rubberised leg.

"Don't listen to a word," his buddy, Jonathan Brandis, says, punctuating this advice with a teenage snicker as he bops by. "Don't listen to a word he says."

Marco Sanchez, the up-and-coming teen heartthrob in his own right, smiles an engaging smile. "Would you like me to talk about the experience of wearing a wetsuit?" he asks politely. "They're hot, they're itchy."

Tell me the first time you heard the word seaQuest?

My agent said, "There's this project, *seaQuest*, comin' up. We'd like you to go read for it. They just called for someone who kind of fits your description."

So I went in on the initial audition, and at that time I hadn't heard the buzz on the show. I hadn't known anything about it. I didn't even know that it was a Spielberg project.

Really? When was this?

That was, I think, some time in February of ninety-three, early on.

Did you have a script?

All I had were a couple of pages, and the pages were simply a scene that I've never seen in any script since. I think it was something that was just written up as an audition piece.

At the top of it, it said Ortiz-slash-O'Neill, and Ortiz is my role and O'Neill is Ted Raimi's part. So they were giving the same piece to actors reading for both parts.

So I worked on the scene, and I went into my audition with [director] Irvin Kershner and [Amblin TV vice president] Phil Segal.

Kersh directed the pilot ... and Phil is the father, I guess, of the show. So I met with these two gentlemen, and I read the scene and they seemed pleased and said, "Okay, thank you."

Two weeks later I was called in for a call-back and it went on from there.

Do you have any sort of life outside of this show now?

Not really. The hours are long and if I didn't enjoy the company of the people that I work with, this would be hell, because it's like working in a cave a lot of the time.

It's sort of like working on a submarine.

It really is.

I've done guest spots in other shows and I've done TV movies, but I've never done a series, so I don't know if that's the experience on other shows ...

Have you got a favourite moment in the show?

It's hard to pin it down to one, because one of the great things about this show is not only meeting and working with Roy Scheider, whose movies I grew up watching, whose work I continue to enjoy, but also meeting the guest stars that they get on the show ...

I never tire of that, that's always exciting. So it's hard to pin it down to one.

Is there something you'd like to see your character do that Ortiz hasn't done yet?

Oh yeah. I don't think we really know this character yet. We know what he does, and that's it. We don't know who he is. He's like me.

I know he looks like you.

He looks a lot like me. He's got a sense of humour, he's got some passion, he's got ambitions, and we really don't know any of those things.

We don't know, you know, what his values are. We don't know what his weaknesses are. We just know that he pushes buttons and he's important on the bridge.

It's kind of pretentious to say it, but I'd like him to become a good role model. You know, as an actor, I get *sooo* sick of going into these auditions where it's the typical street guy, and you gotta do the, you know, "typical street thing".

This is a great opportunity to be a Hispanic and to play a role that is responsible and that speaks clearly. He's also bilingual, you know...

Did you want to act since you were a kid?

I've always fantasised about it ... as far back as ten, eleven years old. I took theatre all throughout junior high, and I took theatre all throughout high school, but not until college, when I enrolled in UCLA and I had to decide on a major, did I say, "Oh, what the hell! Why do I want to sit back when I'm sixty years old and go, 'Man! I wish I would've tried that!'"

Did your parents say, "Oh, you're gonna ruin your life"?

Yeah, my parents are very practical people. You know, they've gotten where they are through hard work, and so it's hard to explain to them.

Acting is a crapshoot. Period ... Whether they're immigrants or not, I can imagine any parents being terrified of their child saying, "I want to be an actor."

When did it turn around?

When they finally saw me on TV. Hah-heh-heh. Now they could elbow the person next to them and say, "That's my boy! The one that you're seeing there."

When I came in just now you were reading *A Brief History of Time*. Are you a physics fan, or are you a science fiction fan?

No ... all throughout college I shied away from the sciences. I despised math, and that's one point where I defer to my character ... But I saw the documentary *A Brief History of Time*. It fascinated me!

It didn't seem so removed from me any more, so that's why I picked up the book. And I love it.

What else do you read?

The Anne Rice books, the vampire books.

I read a lot of plays. Of course, this show gives me a lot to read – there's a new script coming out every week and a half.

How do you find your character?

I simply try to relate to the material.

I assess the circumstances this character comes from, what he's saying and what's said about him, and I take whatever side of me applies to that, relates to that, and I try to enhance it. Also, it's the side of me that's competent and trustworthy and responsible, that's on top of it; I mean, I can be a very scattered person, too.

Do you hear from the fans a lot?

Yeah, this is the first job where I do.

It's really heart-warming to get letters from people in different parts of the country, different walks of life.

And I talk about wanting to be a role model to Latinos, but what's really wonderful is getting letters from all kinds of people.

You know, I got this great letter from this cop in Tennessee, a thirty-eight-year-old father of four ... It's really encouraging. They're watching and they're positive. They wish me well ...

How was the earthquake for you?

Terrifying. I was at home [up by the Hollywood Bowl], lying in bed, and I couldn't figure out what was going on. I thought it was a bomb ...

Half of my house is on a hill and half of it is on stilts, and I thought it'd just go tumbling down the hill. And oddly enough, nothing even fell over and not a crack on the wall. If I weren't an actor who had to be in L.A., I'd get out of L.A.

There's a similar kind of energy, both here at work and throughout the city, as when the riots were going on; just this, this *excitement,* this nervous kind of tension.

It brings people together, but there's an obvious nervousness and it's really apparent on the set.

Boy, anytime anything shakes, everyone just runs for the doors!

You got lights hanging over your head, you got catwalks hanging over your head, you got so much set above your head ...

[But] I love that William Shatner's in this episode.

You learned anything from him?

Oh, I watched him do this scene and he is just a pro, because he can just turn it on and off.

[Snaps his fingers]

It's really hard to get focused on a set because there's so much action going on around you, you know? There's so much movement in your peripheral vision, and it's usually rushed ... but he can just –

[Snap]

do it.

THE SHOOT

Signing on for a one-hour weekly television series is like putting out to sea in a submarine. When your boat sets out, you may have a mission and a timetable, but there are uncharted shoals, matey, and, as any old salt can tell you, there be many dangers far, far beneath the upper deep.

△ △ △ △ △ △

At 4.31 on a pre-dawn January morning, a few scant hours before the *seaQuest DSV* cast and crew resume filming their nineteenth episode, entitled "Hide and Seek", a magnitude 6.8 earthquake strikes Los Angeles. While it isn't the much-anticipated Big One, it certainly is a big one, the worst ever to strike the City of Angels, and the damage and destruction are great.

The following Thursday, even as the city still shakes from reported aftershocks, shooting resumes briefly on a huge soundstage so old that silent films were once shot there. The following day, nervously, they try it again. This time joined by an inquisitive interloper.

The Episode

Even in the twenty-first century, Balkan blood feuds continue to threaten the peace of the world. When Captain Nathan Bridger takes aboard the Butcher of the Balkans, Milos Tezlof [played by guest-star William Shatner], and his traumatised young son, who seems to have a psychic link to Darwin, the *seaQuest* is threatened with destruction.

That's the premise of "Hide and Seek", written by Robert Engels, the show's co-executive producer [who also plays mogul Malcolm Lansdowne in the episode], and directed by Lindsley Parsons III, the show's co-ordinating producer and unit production manager.

The script describes Tezlof as the "worst humanity has to offer ... part soothsayer, part gypsy ... hunter and hunted in the same human skin".

But Bridger, who's been haunted by dreams of the dolphin Darwin and of ... *something* impending, takes the war criminal and his near-autistic son aboard ... over the strong objections of his first officer, Commander Jonathan Ford.

At the same time, young Lucas Wolenczak, Sensor Chief Miguel Ortiz and Lieutenant [J.G.] Tim O'Neill are all working in the science deck moon pool to create a devide that will improve on the vocorder, translating the imagery in which the dolphin communicates into holographic pictures. Meanwhile, Tezlof's enemies, armed with a primitive nuclear device, are closing in.

Captain Bridger, meet Captain Kirk

The two famous actors – one currently the sea-faring captain of the UEO's flagship, the *seaQuest DSV 4600,* as well as, formerly, the reluctant, sea-*fearing* Chief Brody of *Jaws* and the self-destructive artist at the incandescent centre of *All That Jazz,* among many others; the other, the redoubtable first master of the USS *Enterprise* – stand side by side, rehearsing their lines quietly on the futuristic submarine's science-deck set. In the distance a bell sounds.

"Okay, ladies and gentlemen," the first assistant director booms out, "we are on a bell, *on a bell.*"

"*Shake!*" the director yells, and around the monitors crew members laugh nervously, but quietly. "Beam me outa here," says one fervently.

The first A.D. hushes them. It's only four days since the big L.A. quake - not the kind of Hollywood shake-up they're used to around here - but this is show *business;* they're all pros and know that, on the lot, time is money. Big money.

"Ready. And ... *Action!*"

Nathan Bridger, captain of the seaQuest DSV 4600, *leans over the Science Deck dolphin pool and gazes thoughtfully down into Ensign Darwin's intelligent, unblinking eyes. "You brought him here. Why?" he implores.*

"Bring. See-Czar," the petite script supervisor, known in less-enlightened days as the continuity girl, calls out from a dozen feet behind the cameras, straining up on tiptoe and hugging a fat notebook containing the most up-to-the-second revisions in the actors' speeches to her chest, as she enunciates the dolphin's lines, which will be dubbed in later, in post-production.

Bridger studies Darwin as if somewhere in his friend the answer might be floating. Then something seems to pass between them.

A beat. Bridger stands and goes to the door. Opens it to reveal Tezlof and his son, Caesar, there waiting. The boy runs to the edge of the moon pool to see Darwin.

Actor William Shatner, forever identified as Captain James T. Kirk of the starship *Enterprise*, and the curly-haired, solemn-faced young boy who plays his son enter. Made up with a bushy moustache and a politico's paunch, and wearing a grey suit with an open-collared white shirt, he resembles nothing so much as the kind of Israeli politician one sees striding sombrely out of cabinet meetings on the nightly news. He delivers his lines solemnly, befitting the gravity of the scene, so quietly that

the script supervisor again draws herself up on tiptoe, straining to hear.

Bridger
In the dream, Tezlof, who is it that ... is riding on the dolphin? And what ... are you hiding from me?

"Shake!" the off-camera director yells again, as the camera operators' assistants shake the two Panavision cameras, simulating depth charges exploding near the sub.

Tezlof
Too late.

"Cut!"

"Let's do it again!"

"Set it up, guys!"

The set erupts in a buzz of quake-dominated cross-conversation and between-the-takes activity: one of the two cameras is reloaded, a light is adjusted. Everything is readied to replay the brief scene.

"We could do the move a little better," says Kenneth Zunder, the director of photography, of A-camera's movement: a slow pullback, with a little fillip to the side that results in a two-shot – Scheider and Shatner as seen over the dolphin's "shoulder".

"Let's do it once more," the director says.

"Let's do it, please," the first A.D. booms out, in that deep voice cultivated by first assistant directors everywhere.

"Two cameras."

Again, the bell sounds: a kind of insistent, buzzing, rrriiiing that calls kids in from the schoolyard. "Ssshh!"

"We're on a bell! On a bell and a red" – a reference to the red light at each outer door, forbidding entrance to the soundstage while shooting is in progress. "Quiet, please!"

The director takes up his position behind the monitors, dons earphones and, once again, calls out: "And ... *Shake!*"

They run through it again, and again, and again. In between takes, all the conversation is about The Quake and its aftermath. Even L.A. natives, and third generation show-business veterans at that, have never experienced the like; no one has, it's the worst earthquake in the city's history, and soon it will be judged The Most Expensive Natural Disaster In The History Of The United States. But through it all, this crew soldiers on, through the aftershocks, through the tedium of endless repetition. And so goes the day on the Hollywood studio set.

The Earth Rumbles

Everywhere on the giant studio lot there is construction and noise and activity.

Metal-masked welders bend over acetylene torches, carpenters hammer and saw. Trucks and vans rumble through the narrow streeets between soundstages, while entire schools of red-flagged golf carts zip by, dodging pedestrians and messengers on bicycles alike. On the producer's building, a squat formless structure, someone has covered over the earthquake cracks with silvery packing tape.

Another aftershock sends jittery studio workers into their cars, turning the back lot's narrow byways into a scene of temporary gridlock worthy of an L.A. rush hour.

Despite press reports to the contrary, none of *seaQuest*'s expensive standing sets has been damaged. But two of the five soundstages on which the show shoots have sustained structural damage, and sets have to be moved. And when the earth rumbles, the crew – like all crews – grumbles.

"Too much work," says one, exhausted after a fourteen hour day, outside a soundstage that's being demolished. It's the eternal complaint: "Too many hours."

Reminded that he's getting *lots* of overtime, he shoots back: "I'll trade the O.T. for three more hours of sleep. They only give me thirty-six hours off to recuperate on the weekend!"

"Oh, they give you *a whole thirty-six*?" zings another crew member, passing by the former *seaQuest* stage.

"Stage Fourteen. It was fine when we were on it last Friday," the second crew member snorts. "Today, [because of the quake damage] it's coming down."

The Supervising Producer

In the waning afternoon there's a delay. Supervising Producer Les Sheldon has turned up to reassure a group of crew members that, after the morning's three strong aftershocks, the cavernous soundstage is still structurally sound, and that they're safe continuing to work.

"Your feelings and your families come first!" he calls out emphatically, loudly enough so that they can hear him in the distant corners of the stage. "Your feelings and your families come first! He repeats it over and over again, like a mantra, until the skittish crew has calmed noticeably.

One crew member wants to know if any of the aftershocks have released dangerous asbestos onto the set.

"I don't think so," says Sheldon, adding earnestly, "but I'll find out."

Behind him, Shatner turns to Scheider. "Fibre's good for us," he says deadpan.

Laughter defuses the tension, and Sheldon leaves while the crew starts setting up the next shot. Within minutes, before the cameras start rolling again, the first A.D. calls out "Guys! Guys! We've just got a message from Les. He says they checked with Operations and Stage Twenty-Eight has been deemed safe to shoot in.

		Page 5
		Wed, Jan 19, 1994
"HIDE AND SEEK" ONELINE SCHEDULE		
COMPANY MOVE TO SOUND STAGE 28		1/8 pgs.
Scs. 5PT	INT BRIDGE CU ON O'NEIL ID:6	3 3/8 pgs.
Scs. 5,6,7,8,9	INT BRIDGE O'NEIL SLEEPS ON THE BRIDGE ID:6, 7, 12	pgs.
Scs. 9PT	INT UEO OFFICE UEO CALLS FOR GENERAL ALERT ID:12	
End Day #5 -- Total Pages: 6 2/8		
		1 6/8 pgs.
Shoot Day #6 -- Tue, Jan 25, 1994		
Scs. 62,63,64,65	INT BRIDGE HITCHCOCK SAYS THEY ARE LOWERING A NUCLEAR WARHEAD/END OF ACT TWO ID:1, 2, 4, 5, 6, 7, 8, 10	1 2/8 pgs.
Scs. 72	INT BRIDGE BLAST STRIKES SQ AND THE SERB REAPPEARS ID:1, 2, 6, 7, 15	2/8 pgs.
77	INT BRIDGE FORD ORDERS MOONPOOL DOORS CLOSED ID:2, 7	5/8 pgs.
Scs. 81	INT BRIDGE LUCAS TELLS BRIDGER THE KID IS MISSING ID:1, 2, 9	1/8 pgs.
Scs. 86	INT BRIDGE CORRIDOR UNFLOODING GRAPHIC ID:	2/8 pgs.
Scs. 34,36	INT SEADECK/MOONPOOL THEY FLIP THE SWITCHES ID:6, 7, 9	5/8 pgs.
Scs. 35,37,38	INT SEADECK/MOONPOOL DARWIN SAYS THE DREAMER IS COMING ID:6, 7, 9	4/8 pgs.
Scs. 44,45	INT SCIENCE LAB/MOONPOOL LUCAS RIDES DARWIN CAESAR TALKS ID:3, 9, 14	
End Day #6 -- Total Pages: 5 3/8		
Shoot Day #7 -- Wed, Jan 26, 1994		

There's no asbestos in this particular set."

[A week later, when a visitor asks the first A.D. what the atmosphere was like on the set that tense day, with already frayed nerves shaken by strong aftershocks, the A.D. replies that "one of the producers came to the set and spoke and let 'em know that he was with the crew and he was being supportive.

["It helped the morale," the A.D. adds. "He has a genuine respect for his crew and that's important."]

The bell rings. "Bring Darwin in," the director says. On set, production resumes: "Let's roll 'em. Two cameras. A-camera mark, B-camera mark. Ready, and ... "*Shake!*"

△ △ △ △ △ △

Les Sheldon is a big man, who dresses casually in sweaters, jeans and white sneakers – in Hollywood, the creative execu-

tive's uniform of choice – with a voice husky from too many cigarettes.

In fact, on his cluttered production-office desk sit no fewer than four open packs of smokes – Camels, Pall Malls and two more packs of filters.

Meeting a curious visitor, he declares at the outset: "I'm gonna tell you lies," then proceeds to talk passionately about artistic vision and truth.

Asked what a supervising producer does, Sheldon points out – quite correctly – that, in TV, "titles can be very nebulous; it depends on what you bring as an individual with it".

He's writer-oriented, Sheldon allows, and that "drove me into the directing end ... because of my story knowledge and [because of] working with actors".

But television is *the* collaborative medium, and the Sheldon job description touches most of the important production bases:

"In my capacity as supervising producer, I oversee the production creatively ... from taking the first writers' draft and working with the writers on those drafts, those stories and structure, through to the casting of the show ... All the way through to the look of the show and having meetings, which I do every episode, with the production designer, the art director and the set decorator ... to discussions with the guest cast ... and our regular actors, keeping them apprised of where the characters are going, what's happening in each script.

"And what's one of the most important things," Sheldon continues, lighting up, "is getting the guest cast aboard creatively, as far as *who* are they playing, *how* does it fit in to where we're going with the show, *what* are we looking for in the character, because, you know, in a series it happens very quickly."

"Quickly" is an understatement. Every two weeks, during the shooting season, they turn out the equivalent of a feature film. Put another way, in the same amount of time that it will take to shoot and prepare a typical ninety-minute feature film, a one-hour TV series will produce twenty or more hours of programming.

Sheldon's interaction with the current guest star, William Shatner, is typical of the process:

"I had a conversation with [him] at least two weeks before we even started shooting the episode, when we approached him to see if he would do it, and just purely talked to him about the character he'd be playing in the show. There was no script at that point."

So what did he say that caused Shatner to beam aboard? "I talk to them about the show and how the character functions ... and the levels of the character – what's driving him? Forget about what's written on the paper.

"I'm much more interested in *who* they are," Sheldon says emphatically, "not what they do on the show. So, it's what *drives* the human being to become what they are." And that, precisely, is the crux of the interaction in the episode between Shatner's and Scheider's characters.

Bridger
[to Tezlof] I don't know why I let you on this boat. I ... suspect that for some reason we are having ... the same dream. But there are certain images ... in the dream I can't make out. You're going ... to stay here until I do.

Tezlof
You're right. Your dolphin put things in my ... head.

Bridger
You're carrying something inside you that ... I need to know.

"What drives Nathan Bridger is a sense of adventure," the supervising producer continues. "The excitement that goes with that sense of exploring things that have not been explored before, where there may be fear or preconceived notions attached ... Nathan Bridger is the type of guy who wants to find out why you see something differently than I see it, and encompass that in his knowledge, and encompass that in his understanding of the other human being.

"We're dealing with that in this [episode] with William Shatner [who plays] on the surface a very, very misguided human being, and yet Nathan Bridger invites him on the ship.

"People come into Bridger's quarters and want to know, 'Why are you having this evil man come on the ship?' 'So I can get to know what makes him evil.'"

Aha! then what drives Tezlof? "Power," the supervising producer replies without hesitation. And the beautiful Doctor Westphalen? "Compassion."

How about young Lucas, the precocious computer genius? "An inordinate sense of curiosity combined with a balance that he has as a teenager ... that is looked upon as a lack of knowledge by others. He possesses the ability to get and understand and express himself in an arena filled with quote-unquote 'adults'.

"He's a child in an adults' world, yet his instincts drive him and his interests drive him to the same things that those adults are driven to. He brings another view, and yet many times it is interpreted as 'the kid thinks'."

And the supervising producer himself, one wonders, what drives him? "Very much my passion for what you hear me talking about: the human element, humanity, and the lack of it."

The Gatekeeper

Every show has its gatekeeper, whether it's a unit publicist, trying to control the flow of information; an on-location security man, discreetly protecting celebrities from their avid fans; or a producer, guarding that sacrosanct bottom line. So what's *seaQuest*'s gatekeeper, a back-slapping old timer who's made it his mission to "protect" the shoot from inquiring minds, got to be worried about?

"That's easy enough to explain," offers an insider who's savvy about these things. "It's not politically correct to be talking about this, but first off, it's the money 'cause it's *always* the money, and we're talkin' a *million-five* a negative."

A "negative" is Hollywood shorthand for a single episode.

"And Roy's not happy and Steven's not happy, and there's the Big Darwin Secret."

True, but all that's already been in the press: the ultra-realistic, high-tech dolphin model has even been praised publicly by animal rights people; you can't buy publicity like that.

What's more, when kids are working on the set, they're asked to raise their right hands and swear to keep the Darwin Secret, and as a reward they each get to spend a few seconds with the high-tech dolphin model – and even though ten- and eleven-year-olds have just been let in on the Big Secret, "they pet and kiss and talk to the mechanical dolphin just like it was the real thing; it's really touching," says one awed crew member.

As for earthquakes, in one sense, *seaQuest* has already had it's own, and auteur Steven Spielberg, commendibly forthright, whose TV company produces the show, has said in print that he wished there'd been more time to prepare before going on air, and that henceforth the series would concentrate more on stories about *character* – just as lead-actor Roy Scheider – who also says he wants the series to move to Florida, so he won't have to put his family through another season in earthquake country – would like.

The result of the Spielberg and Scheider tremors on *seaQuest* has been the addition of a hot new group of writer/producers, whose mandate is to put the show back on creative course.

"It was not a show that I either created or was in at the ground floor on," says David J. Burne, one of the new executive producers, whose reputation is in character-based drama as his credits attest. I came in and there were a myriad of problems that were not mine, that were the result of the best intentions of decent people."

Asked to summarise those problems, Burke says: "It was inexperience, people in certain key positions; it was the lack of viewpoint on the show by people who were actually running it

... There was an inability to communicate with Roy, who's the star. It is really *essential* that the executive producer and the star get along with each other and communicate."

The insider shrugs. "Then there are all the actors and all the producers, especially the new guys, everybody angling for the spotlight."

But if all that's already been in the press – Darwin, the staff changes, the actors' complaints – what's with the Gatekeeper, anyway? He's continually trying to shunt the visitor away to the most innocuous parts of the production, places like the video playback room which, in reality, is an interesting and crucial, part of the shoot.

"Hey, get over it," shrugs the insider. "It's Hollywood, whadya expect?"

The Video Playback Room

"*seaQuest* is a video-intensive show," says Christopher A. Blodgett, one of the men in the video playback room.

One day when all that video equipment powers up and trips a circuit breaker on set, he loyally, and rather hilariously, blames it on the coffee pot at craft-services [as the snack table is known in show-biz parlance].

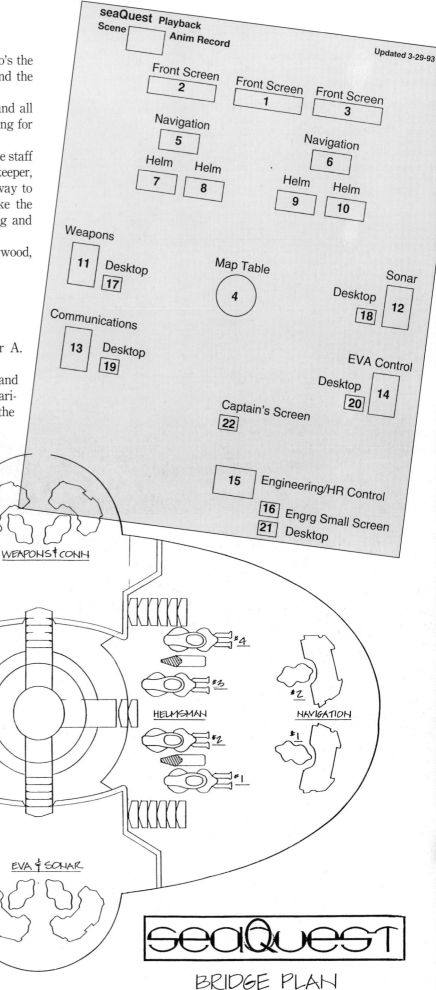

Most of the video playback originates in a small window-less room in a corner of vast soundstage twenty-eight.

"We do a lot of videophones, when somebody communicates to somebody on a visual phone," says Ben Betts, another of the video-playback stalwarts, eyeing a black-and-white monitor on which actor Don Franklin [Commander Jonathan Ford] is rehearsing a scene in front of the hologram "waterfall". "We send computer graphics all over to different screens around the *seaQuest*. [We do the displays for] hand-held computers, little laptop computers. Basically, any type of display on the ship we are responsible for."

They create different graphics for each episode in video playback, relying on basic "wallpaper" displays for the more general background screens.

"When they need something different quickly, we just kind of create it here on the spot. We can do multiple overlays and kind of patch things together," says Betts. "The typical problem is, they want something at the last minute, and we had no preparation."

The small black-and-white Sony monitor showing the smoky waterfall is patched into the viewfinder of one of the Panavision cameras. "That way we can match, when actors are supposed to be pressing buttons, to make sure the screen changes at the appropriate time. The hologram is actually a sheet of smoke, with clean air on either side of it, and then we project with a video projector onto the smoke.

"We've got who we call the Professor, who plays normally in the captain's quarters, and we actually shoot that with a live camera and an actor," Betts explains. "Supposedly the Professor is a computer-generated image. We do it all real time. Right now [in this scene], the [hologram] unit's not supposed to be working, so I'm feeding it either white or black. I could also send in a graphic or a videotape element or a computer-generated element.

"We have one-and-a-half gigabyte hard drive that we constantly have to back up; we've filled it completely with animations."

In addition to the broadcast quality betacam and three-quarter-inch videotape decks in playback, there's a dynamic tracking deck, which can do slow or fast motion, and up to nine computers, each with a graphic display. Ideas for the imagery they deploy come from film, magazines, television and science fiction.

In one episode, says Betts, "We had eighty-six different playback elements. For example, *Jurassic Park* had twelve. In one episode we actually had eighty-six different images.

"When I say twelve elements or eighty-six elements, that's a different graphic that'll appear on the screen at some point."

Up to twenty-two of those images can appear at any one time on the bridge set itself, which has that many working screens – the three biggest, Barco 5000s, cost fifty-five thousand dollars each. "Every one of those screens has to have a different image on it. All of those images have to be co-ordinated and set up in this room."

Because all that imagery flies by so quickly – and because the work is done at such a rapid pace that there's even no time for the director to approve each and every image – there's the usual craftperson's opportunity for inside jokes. Says Betts: "Oftentimes it'll be random numbers [generated] but we put [on screen] people's birthdays and initials and all sorts of things where people [watching at home] can't read them."

Video Dating in the Twenty-First Century

Another day, another scene. Crowding the science deck set are eighteen production crew members. A stagehand weaves through the crowd carrying a ladder that he climbs to adjust an overhead light, while below the D.P. peers through the Panavision camera.

It's a rehearsal for the brief scene in which Captain Bridger joins Commander Ford and Chief Crocker [Royce Applegate] in front of a video screen on one of the sea decks. On screen, making a videophone call is Doctor Westphalen [Stephanie Beacham], saying, "I am sorry, Nathan, I had no choice but to make this call," then, ominously, she steps out of frame and a scowling Milos Tezlof, the Butcher of the Balkans, appears.

Roy Scheider strolls in, in one hand a styrofoam cup steaming with coffee; in the other a lollypop. He draws a slew of appreciative snickers from the crew by delivering his first lines – "What's wrong?" – with a Yiddish accent:

"Vot's wrong?" asks Bridger, to which Royce Applegate, who plays the crusty security chief, shoots back: "Is this a tribute to Telly Savalas?" The crew guffaws.

Scheider gives Applegate an arch look and they both laugh, just as the frowing William Shatner is projected on the video – "Hello," he says with a slight middle-European accent.

"Is this a dating service?" Scheider quips. The crew, which doesn't miss much, loves these kinds of snide remarks and laughs heartily.

"Two minutes," an A.D. calls out, as the grips and gaffers rush to finish setting up. "Places for picture. Awright ... a bell and red."

"Playback, you're re-cued and standing by? Okay, let's shoot."

The Script Supervisor

"Basically, what I do is make sure everything is consistent from shot to shot," says the *seaQuest* script supervisor, a diminutive young woman with a halo of frizzy hair framing a perpetually quizzical expression, "so it all looks like it happened at the same time."

Susan Lowitz, a ten-year veteran, is almost always at the elbow of the director or the D.P., or in shouting range of the actors to feed them their lines. It's late in the shoot, but the scene about to get under way comes early in the story, so she has to make certain that the dialogue and action in the scene are consistent with everything that came before, and that it flows consistently into what will come after.

But more often, she says, issues of consistency are internal, within a scene. "If Roy is wearing his glasses and takes them off in the middle of a scene, I make sure he takes them off on the same line with the same hand [in every take] so, if they cut from one angle to another, if our esteemed editors do that, then they'll be able to do that without his glasses jumping from his face to his hand, or vice versa. There's a shot in the first *Star Trek* movie where William Shatner's glasses jump on and off his face. It's kinda fun."

Often, actors vary their lines slightly from take to take. "I keep a record of the variations," she says. "If it's anything that's not close to what the line should be, then I'll tell them."

It's all in her big book, filled with script pages and their variants, all coded according to a system recognised by the editors, who eventually will assemble a very rough cut of the episode out of the jumble of shots and takes. She opens it up to a typical script page, covered with wavy vertical lines, stick figure icons and annotations. "This is the scene we just did: it's Lucas, O'Neill, Ortiz and Bridger talking on sea deck." The stick figures?

"Yah, that's so I can record the position they're sitting in, so that [the actors] know which knee they had up, and things like that." And the squiggly lines, the straight vertical lines and the hand-drawn circles?

Each circle represents a camera doing a specific kind of a shot. On this shoot, there are usually two Panavision cameras recording each take. "So the squiggly line means that whatever [it] was over was *not* on camera for that particular shot. It could be on an actor's back ... or they could not be in frame at all, and that tells the editor either they can let in another line [of dialogue] or they'll wanna look for a straight line [on the script page] which indicates that the person was on camera, so that they can cut to *that* shot. It's an old system, I didn't make it up."

seaQuest presents one special problem for the script supervisor. "One being that ... we use a lot of video [on the various screens and monitors, and in special effects]. We do a lot of video playback on the bridge; we do a lot of telephone conversations via the vidlink. Needless to say, we shoot that half in one place and half in the other. I end up doing a lot of off-screen dialogue ..."

She also doubles for Darwin, whose dialogue is dubbed in later, in post-production. "Darwin's fun, and his lines are short so they're easy to memorise."

The Pros

"Okay, let's do a rehearsal, please!" a disembodied voice booms out. It's another short scene – a two-shot from over Roy Scheider and William Shatner's shoulders.

"Rehearsing!"

"All right, quiet guys!"

"Ssshh!"

They run through it, casually as usual. Shatner, whispering his lines so they're barely audible; Scheider rushing through his. They're two pros; each seemingly at ease, but wrapped in a sphere of concentration that excludes not only the other actors and the crew, but the whole rest of the world. Energy and focus seem to be what they're conserving. After the rehearsal come the takes, and they're nothing like the perfunctory rehearsals. Shatner and Scheider make the words spark with portent and drama.

The director and the D.P. watch the actors on the two black-and-white Burle monitors, one for each camera, which see what the Panavision cameras see. On each monitor screen a hair's width outline traces the "frame" of the home viewers' TV sets. With taped "marks" on the floor, the actors should be positioned perfectly, but on take one, which is otherwise flawless, Shatner is just a half-step too far to the side.

At the monitor, D.P. Zunder taps the screen as if he could move him to his mark by sheer willpower. Next to him, director Parsons laughs.

"Cut! ... That would've been good," he mutters, calling out, "Bill, would you step about two inches to your left?"

They do it again, and again. After the third take, the director nods approvingly. "Good for you, Ken!"

The D.P. shakes his head from side to side. "Needs a touch-up."

Parsons shrugs. "Let's do it again."

After the fourth take, the D.P. is frowning. "It's always the easy shots," he shrugs. And they quickly run through it yet again.

Finally, they get it. There's a wave of relieved laughter from the crew. "Okay, coverage. Turning around! This is two cameras." Around come the cameras for reaction shots: a two shot, then a close-up of Scheider. As they work, somebody's whistling the theme from Gilligan's Island. "Hey," says a wag, "GilliganQuest."

Actor John D'Aquino, who plays the acerbic Lieutenant Benjamin Krieg, comes bopping past. "KriegQuest," is all he says.

It's a ...

They've moved to the bridge set at the centre of venerable soundstage twenty-eight, where the classic 1925 silent horror film, *The Phantom of the Opera*, was filmed. The interior of the grand opera house from that movie, which starred Lon Chaney Sr., the "man of a thousand faces", still stands – ornate, ghostly greyish white; the opera boxes like skeletal eyes – and at its centre is the *seaQuest* bridge.

The real-life effect is eerie and reminiscent of the mysterious movie moment near the end of *2001,* when the twenty-first century Jupiter probe space pod comes to rest in the middle of an elegant, Louis XIV-furnished room.

The bridge set itself is gunmetal-grey and dark, illuminated video screens and computer consoles. Unlike the bright and blue-water feel of the submarine's science deck, this is a place of momentous action, of potential war.

Quickly, the actors run through another rehearsal for the scene in which Lieutenant Commander Hitchcock [Stacy Haiduk] tells the Captain that an object – something like a wrecking ball – is being lowered toward them.

Ortiz
Any number of craft directly above us, sir. They range from gunboats to small recon vessels to large fishing trawlers. They were using some sort of primitive jamming system on our communications buoy ...

Another scrape.

Bridger
Who's doing the scraping?
(off another noise)
What is the scraping?
Hitchcock works on the HR probe.

Hitchcock
(complete disbelief)
Captain, they've apparently lowered what ... looks to be a wrecking ball.

Bridger
A wrecking ball?

Hitchcock
Check that, sir. Not a wrecking ball ...
She hesitates to go on.

Bridger
What?

But on this set, and with this leading man, rehearsals aren't just for emoting. They're for doing vaudeville shtik, and you can practically hear the rimshots:

Again the tremulous-voiced Lieutenant Commander Katherine Hitchcock, at her virtual-reality console in one corner of the bridge: "They've apparently lowered ... something ... something that looks like a wrecking ball ..."

The "wrecking ball" is coming closer and closer to the ship. Scheider fairly bounds onto the set. "Vot eez it?" he asks, in a voice that's pure Catskills comic.

"C'mon: *everybody!*" yells Stacy Haiduk ebulliently, and like some manic game-show audience answering along with a prize-proclaiming host, the entire cast, and most of the crew, shout back in unison: "It's a ... *Nuclear Warhead*!!!" The cast and crew alike dissolve in helpless, tension-relieving laughter. "Get us outa here!" Scheider, suddenly straight-faced, barks commandingly into the manic gale. After all, it *is* the next line in the script.

△ △ △ △ △ △

Any special problems dressing *this* set, an inquisitive visitor wants to know, gesturing at the elaborate, expensive construction that simulates the battle deck of the futuristic nuclear submarine. Replies the set dresser with a shrug: "Just the same mass confusion you get on every set."

The Stand-in

Marte Post, a fair-complexioned blonde, stands five feet and one inch tall, but she "stands-in" for Doctor Westphalen [Stephanie Beacham] and Lucas Wolenczak [Jonathan Brandis] when camera angles are being planned and shots are being lighted.

Lest you think, "Gee, he doesn't look that tiny on the TV" allow Miz Post to explain: "Neither of them are my height, but I've worked with the cinematographer, Kenny Zunder, for a coupla years before, and he was more interested in people who do the job well, and you can always make adjustments for height, [skin] colours, etcetera."

So, inevitably, Miz Post, who also has acted professionally in such television shows as *Lou Grant* and *The Waltons*, has her boxes. "Yes, I have a box that I'll stand on in case I have to be taller."

And, yes, there *is* a Stephanie box and a Jonathan box. "They have their own little personalities. I run and get them when I know what character I'm going to have to take care of."

From her unique perch – make that, perches – Miz Post has learned a lot about directing and photography and the other televisual arts and crafts, including acting itself. "Some people go into their lines and draw from that," she observes. "Some people have to fix the dialogue to work for them. There are many different systems and techniques. As an example, Roy is an excellent actor and he has great instincts. And from watching, I've learned [that] he's not acting, he's re-acting. He can do anything."

And the secret of successful standing-in? "It's to pay attention and to make the cinematographer's job as easy as possible." And, of course, because the lights that are being adjusted are so bright, "it is advisable to close your eyes".

△ △ △ △ △ △

"Stand by to go again. Two cameras! ... And a bell and a red. And ... *background!* ... And *cut!*"

For once, the brief scene is just ... *perfect*. The director and the cinematographer exchange weren't-nothin'-to-it shrugs.

"Guys, let's set up for rehearsal. Scene sixty-four."

The Mixer

The production sound mixer, Will Yarbrough, is a courtly gentleman who does all the show's dialogue recording. To all appearances, he's a calm and patient man, who cares about his craft. Most days he's to be found off to the side of the main action, seated behind a moveable cart on which is a small

sound board, a black-and-white monitor and a time-code Nagra reel-to-reel sound recorder.

On location – from time to time the entire company decamps for a beachfront shoot in Malibu, not far from Stephanie Beacham's house – the only real sound problem is the surf, he says.

"You never can get a constant level for the dialogue ... We have to use the type of microphone appropriate to the situation, then we have to E.Q. it [i.e. equalise the sound level] without messing up the post-production end of it. If I get [the sound] too thin on the production end, they have nothing to work with when they get to the dubbing stage."

Back on set, "it's business as usual, but this is a very unusual show," he explains, "because we record all *on*stage dialogue, as well as *off*stage dialogue, and sometimes on a set we have as many as eight to nine people talking [in a single scene]. "Therefore, they're gonna film this and I got to mike all these people without getting my microphones in the scene."

He does it with radio microphones that have no wires, as well as "hardwire lavaliers", the kind of unobtrusive clip microphones that one regularly sees worn by newsreaders. "I can only use that [i.e. the lav mikes] if they're not moving around."

On another day, on another set on yet another soundstage, the mixer is not quite so sanguine. Perpetually noisy stagehands have exhausted his patience.

"Quiet! Quiet, goddamnit!" he shouts. "Just 'cause *you're* done with *your* job doesn't mean I'm done with mine!"

A second A.D. hurries over. "Where's the noise coming from?" he asks solicitously.

"All over," huffs the sound mixer, who ought to know, pulling his earphones down around his neck. The grand backhanded wave of his arm takes in every corner of the crowded, noisy stage.

Setting up on the Bridge

What's coming up, says Kenneth Zunder, the director of photography, is a "pretty wide shot of the bridge. We're gonna see up to Ortiz's station, and a little bit of heroic foreground with Roy and Crocker there about to get under attack."

Even here, on the edge of the bridge set – maybe especially here – it's easy to confuse the actors with their roles: "Roy" is, of course, Roy Scheider, the actor who portrays Captain Nathan Bridger, while "Crocker" is Chief Crocker, the character portrayed by actor Royce Applegate.

First, the D.P. says, he will "light the bridge", then set the cameras up for a "pull-in", as Scheider enters, because "there's a sense of urgency".

"They were on the sea deck and got a warning: 'Come to the bridge right away!' It helps the urgency of the scene. Instead of just laying back and having him come at us, we'll push [in] with him. There's a map table in the foreground here, so we'll rush by the foreground [table] and that'll help sell the feeling of urgency."

So the scene will require a "master", or group, shot. "Then we'll cover the people who have dialogue [to have] inter-cuts with. Then, [Admiral] Noyce who we're going to set-up on a set

over here and light it, then do a video feed to this screen [on the bridge] so he appears on this screen live. The actors can actually act with the guy on the screen, as opposed to a blue screen, where you act to a blue screen and they put him in later."

Like many of the other standing sets, the bridge is a "practical set", meaning that it doesn't easily disassemble to accommodate camera moves and angles. "The ribs [of the sub] don't move, we got two different levels. This shot happens to be all on one level, so we lucked out ... The camera's gonna end up right next to this [structural] rib, so the [camera] operator [who actually sits behind the camera] is gonna be hanging on with two toes ..."

It's all done in the interest of verisimilitude; even the set floors, which after all are rarely if ever seen on TV, are the kind of grating – hard to manoeuvre over – found in an actual submarine. "That's why it's here ... It's like a practical [i.e. real] location. And we have a lot of exposed guts, which I think are nice. I mean, there's a lot of beauty to this set, a lot of grace."

A grip carrying a long piece of heavy wood to lay as dolly track for the camera comes weaving past on the crowded set. "Over here," the D.P. says to his interlocutor, "stand next to me. You know he's not going to hit me." The grip laughs, but gives the D.P. a wide berth.

"Anyway," Zunder continues, "to me there's a lot of contrast on this sub. It's very graceful, it's almost like a cathedral." Truly, with its curving arches and high domed ceiling the bridge set does have that aspect. "Yet, there's a lot of metal,

we've got exposed guts under those grates ... This sub has a little bit of everything."

The bridge is mostly military grey. "To break up the monotony of the walls, I add a lot of colour [with lights]. The up lights are often blue; the graphics are often blue on the screen, so [the lights] are mimicking the colours that are on the screens. When the [instrument] panels are lit up, they're often amber in tone, so [other lights] are imitating that on the walls. So if you're looking around, it's not just all grey sub, you've got little splashes of colour here and there."

B-Camera

B-camera, like A which gets the master shot, is a Panaflex Gold by name. It, too, usually, has one thousand feet of Kodak film in its magazine.

For, say, ten minutes of shooting time just the unprocessed film stock itself costs approximately four hundred and fifty dollars. To process it runs about forty-five cents per foot. The total then for each thousand-foot magazine is roughly nine hundred dollars.

B-camera isn't used very often, but if it results in three or four usable shots per day, it's paid for itself, according to the D.P. rule of thumb.

As the bridge is being readied for the next scene, through the clutter of workmen and the cacophony of cross-conversation, Craig Asato, second assistant on B-camera, sees the moment through a visitor's eyes: "If you stand out here and just kind of look over it impassively, it's kind of like ants building an ant hill. It rarely makes a lot of sense. Everybody is screaming; they're throwing things around."

As if to prove the point, the D.P. calls out: "We need a troy to hide the pepper," which, says Asato, roughly translated means: "Troy is [the name of] the big electrician, and 'troy' is [also] a piece of black [cloth] they can use to hide the pepper," which is a small light overhead.

The Dress Rehearsal

The bell rings, for the umpteenth time this day.

"Ssshh …"

"Quiet for rehearsal!"

"Ladies and gentlemen, we're on a bell. Please stop talking. This'll be a full rehearsal, guys."

"Okay?"

"Okay. Now, let's take it from the entrance just to see how it works. Okay, background, just be a little further back. Where're you guys looking?"

The "background" – that is, the extra, who is an actor with no lines – points in answer to the director of photography's question. The background's puzzled – after all, he doesn't have any lines, he's just there to fill up the ship's complement – and

he's too new to the game to know, but where he's looking *does* matter.

It's a question of lighting: if he's looking one way in rehearsal and then even a slightly different way when the cameras are rolling, his face will be lighted improperly.

"Quietly, please."

"*Quietly!*"

"So here we go," says the director, "just to get into it: Roy has just said, on the sea deck, 'What the hell's going on?' And Stacy [Haiduk, who plays Lieutenant Commander Hitchcock, replies] 'I'm not sure, sir.' That's where we'll start. Ready … And: 'What the hell's going on?'"

"I'm not sure, sir," replies the young actress, her features practically invisible behind her virtual-reality goggles.

The actor who plays Admiral Noyce has come to the edge of the set in mid-make-up – a small towel still covering his shirtcollar – to "throw" Scheider lines, but he's a half-beat behind the rhythm of the dialogue. The director prompts him: "And Noyce says, 'Tezlof's enemies …'"

Noyce
Tezlof's enemies have found him. They want you to give him up for execution.

Bridger
(quizzically)
How'd they find him?

Noyce

On the information superhighway there's lots of hitch-hikers. Lots of people there before it was built.

"And ... Scrape!" calls out the director, watching at the monitors. Later, the special effects will be put in.

Bridger

(in command)
Dive!
(to Ortiz)
What is this?

Ortiz

Any number of craft directly above us, sir. They range from gunboats to small recon vessels to large fishing trawlers. They were using some sort of primitive jamming device. I was slow to recognise it. Identify it. Sorry, sir.

"Scrape!" shouts the director.

Bridger

Who's doing that scraping?

As Scheider delivers the line, the focus puller, who measures distances from camera to actors, runs a tape measure from B-camera right up to the tip of his nose.

Hitchcock

(complete disbelief)
Captain, they've apparently lowered what looks to be a wrecking ball.
(a beat)
Check that, sir. It's not a wrecking ball. It's ... a nuclear warhead!

Bridger

Get us out of here!

"Okay, that's our cut on rehearsal!"
"Get us outa here."
"Very funny."
"Ssh! Ssh-ssh-ssh!"
"Let's do some work on 'scrape'. React to it!" The director walks over to the B-camera operator. "Same deal," he says. "When you hear 'scrape', camera shake."

"Okay, this'll be another rehearsal! Stand by! ... Rehearsal bell, please."

It rings, and they go through it again – vidscreen admirals, wrecking balls, nukes, scrapes and shaking cameras. Afterwards, a grip brings an eight-foot ladder up to the centre of the set and quickly scrambles up to adjust an overhead light: another one of the actors has changed the direction of his gaze and now has to be re-lighted. Finally, they go to picture and seem to get it in two quick takes.

"Excellent," says the director after take two, and the D.P. agrees – "it was a beauty" – but ... one of the actor's lavalier

mikes has fallen off, so as soon as the two cameras are reloaded ... they go through it once again.

The Boom Man

Standing on the upper level of the bridge deck and straining back to handle the extended bent pole, David Sanucci could be a fisherman, with a big one on the line, but he is the boom mike operator [or microphone placement engineer, as he once described himself on a bank-loan application], and his job is holding microphones over actors' heads, but he's also "reponsible for watching the set-ups of the scenes and then determining how [to] attack ... to get all the dialogue [recorded]".

It's those *practical* sets that create his difficulties, too – mikes have to be hidden, built-in structural elements that don't fly [i.e. don't move] have to be accommodated.

For the second act-ending, it's-a-nuclear-warhead scene they're using a "combination of boom mikes, plant mikes and lavalier mikes. Boom mikes being the hand-held overhead mikes, plant mikes being ones that we hide behind something and a lavalier, which will be the body-type mike ... Often, we'll have three, four, five mikes working in a scene."

Once those microphones are in place, though, the mixer, at his off-set soundboard, wields ultimate authority over the levels at which they're set.

The boom mike Sanucci's holding is on a flexible carbon-fibre pole, actually called a fishpole, that is extendable out to eighteen feet. Where he holds it depends on the lens that's on the Panaflex.

The position of the microphone is determined by "what millimetre lens," he says. "If you're shooting a twenty-four millimetre lens at, say, six feet, I have to be [at a certain height] to be out of the picture. Now, if they do a close-up, and put a hundred millimetre or an eighty-five millimetre lens [on], then the amount of room between the top of the head and the top of the frame line is decreased, and I can get much closer."

How does he know how close he can get without becoming visible? Practice let's him eyeball it. "You have to know your lenses," he adds. "Tools of the trade."

△ △ △ △ △ △

Another day, another soundstage on the sprawling lot: the crew is setting up for the big engine-room confrontation between Bridger and Tezlof. It's the first time they've shot on the engine-room set, all pipes and tanks and exotic flashing lights, courtesy of video playback, which – although they genially deny it – is today packing so much electronic hardware that when they first power-up, they promptly blow a fuse.

The Second A.D.

Brash, in-your-face New Yorker may not be part of the job description (although the experience obviously helps), but for Matthew T. Weiner, key second assistant director, it is an essential element of his on-the-job style. "Coming from New York, I'm very used to an aggressive style as a second," he says directly – and rapidly. What he does is "mostly middle management, as far as implementing and enforcing the executive producer's, the director's [and] the first assistant director's directives.

"Basically, I'm like the line sergeant," he explains, "I'm the guy who makes sure the troops have their information.

"There's a creative aspect to this job," Weiner adds, "which they've allowed me a lot of latitude with.

"I direct background [i.e. extras] ... You know, give me a thousand people and I can get some wild things going for you. And they've given me a total free hand on this job, which I really, really enjoy.

"They tell me the numbers [of extras], I bring them in. My first day in this job ... I walked on and said, 'What do you want with the background?' [The director said:] 'We hear you're an artist. Paint.'"

The second A.D. has The Speech, well rehearsed, with which he greets the extras, telling them they're the "tapestry on which the principal actors perform". First, he welcomes them to the show,then he explains the scene they'll be "background" for and tells them he's not from California – "not that I have anything against California, or that I have anything against my fellow DGA [Directors Guild of America] members ... but I'm very insistent in my ways and I'm very stubborn in my ways ... I don't want cattle and I don't want stiffs. If I did, I'd go to the morgue or the stockyards. I want actors.

"Then I start getting into it: I explain about the UEO; I explain a brief history of what's happened in the future; [I explain] the fact that they're in the flagship of the UEO, that they all fought ... to get on *seaQuest*, that there's pride in every step that they take.

"We had one scene where the ship is being bombarded by depth-charges, and I have nine extras ... I make sure to tell them: "You're sub-mariners, you're not scared when the ship gets rocked ... you're determined, you go where you're going." I usually can get most of the stuff featuring extras in one take, and directors like that."

The second A.D. counts himself supremely lucky to be in California, "living a New York boy's dream – working for Steven Spielberg. My friends back in New York" – his voice lowers to an awed whisper – "they all say, 'one of us made it into the palace.'"

The second A.D. also specialises in choreographing military moves and his most artistic moment came in an episode called "The Stinger".

"The director kinda looks at me and says, 'Give me somethin' cool,' and I say, 'Oh, I'll give ya somethin' cool.'

"So [Security Chief] Crocker walks in to talk to the bad guy saying, 'We can do this one of two ways: We can do it the easy way ... or we can do it the hard way.'

"And out of *nowhere,* literally, appears seven guys with guns! Just come outa nowhere! One guy comes up from behind him; guys just fold outa nowhere.

"The first time the actors saw it, they had to cut, because they didn't expect it. Just these guys appear outa nowhere – it was like ... *liquid death*!"

Has he studied the martial arts, someone who's been watching his hand movements wants to know. Several years

of Tae Kwan Do, says the second A.D., spinning his Motorola walkie-talkie the way Old West TV gunfighters spin their Colts.

How about a military background? "I live in New York. I figure that's enough."

$$\triangle \ \triangle \ \triangle \ \triangle \ \triangle \ \triangle$$

Near the new engine-room set on stage twenty-three, an excited extra, a young woman in a blue UEO jumpsuit, buttonholes a stranger to proudly display Angela Lansbury's autograph and a snapshot, taken only moments before, of herself standing beaming next to the star of *Murder, She Wrote*. Her hero, she says blissfully.

One of the abiding ironies of the television industry is that competing series, airing opposite each other on competing networks, can be – and are – produced by the same studio. So, despite the the fact that *seaQuest* is "aimed straight at Angela Lansbury's heart", as actress Stephanie Beacham puts it, the fact is that it's only a short walk from the soundstage where *Murder* shoots to where *seaQuest* is filming.

$$\triangle \ \triangle \ \triangle \ \triangle \ \triangle \ \triangle$$

It's another day on another episode, and there's an extra spring to the second A.D.'s New York street bop.

A grip notices it, too. "You been chewin' everybody out today," he remarks blithely in passing.

"A.D.s are five 'n' oh today," the second A.D. replies happily. "Five 'n' oh." Later, he explains just what he means:

"Okay." He ticks it off on his fingers. "I had casting agents who were doing our extras casting [who] decided to send us ten extra kids they weren't supposed to. Now the thing is, the problem with California [is] very strict child welfare and labour laws. Ten kids were sent to me; I had no facilities to educate 'em and I'm not gonna let 'em be dumped off on me. I then took it upon myself to explain this piece of legal obligation to the agents – [They] had to pay salaries and the agents were responsible for the teacher. The kids at this point were truants, so you couldn't send them back to their own school. I then had Central Casting's legal department call me and praise me: "Thank God you knew to do this!" So the ... agent who did this, he basically got screwed and has to eat the cost for being *stupid*.

"We walked in here this morning, because of the earthquake and I'm *totally* sympathetic to what Universal's going through, but I walked into the stage and it's totally covered with dust! ... I don't think so!

"So basically I discussed with [the Operations department] what can or cannot be done, and I won that battle, and no one wins with Operations. I even got them to pay for two additional security guards [to quiet outside construction while shooting was going on inside].

"Operations behaved very professionally; I have my needs, they have theirs. The needs can be met.

"Then it turns out Central Casting forgot to call [in] some of our [other] extra performers. At this point, I was so yelled out, I just called and said, 'Are you going to clean house or shall I come over and do it?' They said [fearfully], 'No, no. We'll take care of everything.'

"That was about it, but it was a good day, because all these little annoyances, we just won. We A.D.s couldn't lose today."

The First Assistant Director

"In layman's terms, I run the show," says Frank Davis, one of the two first assistant directors on *seaQuest*. "I'm the director's assistant and I do whatever I can do to help the director concentrate on his vision."

That means he spends most of his time being a politician, the deep-voiced Davis says with a laugh, "trying to be mellow. It's very important to be mellow. My mentor Jerry Ziesmer taught me that."

He spends his days "scheduling, accommodating the actors when they have other things to do and being able to adjust the schedule so we can continue to move at a swift pace and not be slowed down as a result of that. And also staying in the parameters of whatever budget I may have for my extras, so far as how many extras I'm allotted for the episode."

On the episode shooting this day, "accommodating the actors" means taking into consideration the publicity blitz that guest star William Shatner is mounting for the mini series based on his novel, *TekWar*. "We found out about two days

before he was going to shoot that he wasn't available [on the days he originally was scheduled] ... So we were glad to do whatever we could do to help him out.

"It was also very difficult in many ways 'cause we just had this massive earthquake, and it's a balance of not pushing the crew too hard, because, you know, they have personal things that they're dealing with, but also pushing 'em to a point where we continue to get work done."

Like any video field general, the Chicagoan carries a walkie-talkie and wears a headset. "I'm communicating with my support staff," he explains. "I have a key second assistant director and a second second [assistant director], and after I schedule the show, I give them the shooting schedule, which basically breaks down all the elements, like special equipment, i.e. additional cameras, additional crew personnel ... the development of a particular prop that we might shoot out of order, so they know what the continuity is, listing the day breaks ... They can, in turn, take all that information and pass it on to all the support departments, like wardrobe, so they can make sure everyone has what they need to have."

Davis is what's known as a "rotating first", which means that while he's shooting, his counterpart, John T. Kretchmer, is "prepping" the next episode. When Kretchmer's episode shoots, Davis in turn will be prepping. "So when I finish this episode, I'll be goin' in to get a new script, and I'll be breakin' the script down, and I'll start the whole process over."

When he first sees that new script, Davis looks for such things as special lighting effects, whether minors will be on the set, if the episode will require stuntwork, and which actors will be in which scene.

Davis got into the business while in school, answering phones at the production office of a movie company shooting on his college's campus. When a commercial company from Los Angeles came to the campus, he was experienced enough to get more work, eventually telling the out-of-towners that someday he'd see them in Tinseltown itself.

Later, when he showed up in the movie capital, he called his old commercial buddies: "Some of the people gave me real phone numbers, some of the numbers I dialled were disconnected." One actor, away in Europe, gave him the use of his apartment.

Despite nearly two months of unemployment, he eventually started working. "One thing led to another." He started doing more commercials. The commercials led to another movie, this time as a production assistant. The movies led to more movies – pictures like *Twins, Rising Sun* and *Terminator II*, and the road from P.A. eventually led to A.D. – "I was a sponge and tried to learn as much as I could," he says. He now plans to direct and produce.

Interrupted by the earthquake, Lindsley Parsons III, co-ordinating producer on *seaQuest,* is finally coming to the end of directing his first episode of the show.

While waiting for his guest star, he's explaining to a visitor that when the big quake hit, he didn't think about the show, or the possible delays or the damage at all. It was his parents, who live near the epicentre, that he was concerned about and he immediately drove to them.

Director Parsons' recollection is interrupted by the guest star, William Shatner, who at first asks to be reminded of just what scene they're supposed to be doing, and then he does it in one take – to the vocal appreciation of the crew.

Like the old pro he is, Shatner takes the scattered applause and whistles in stride, holding up a restraining hand. "I know, I know," he says to the applauding crew in that familiar caramelly rich voice. "You wanna clean your houses up. I can see that." Then he strides away.

"Wow," whispers one crew member, "it's like a *Star Trek* convention around here." And indeed, the guest star has been signing autographs all week, and the staff stills photographer has been button-holed many times by crew members wanting him to pose for photos with them or, as shyly as any tourist, they ask him to autograph his glossies, or they just ask

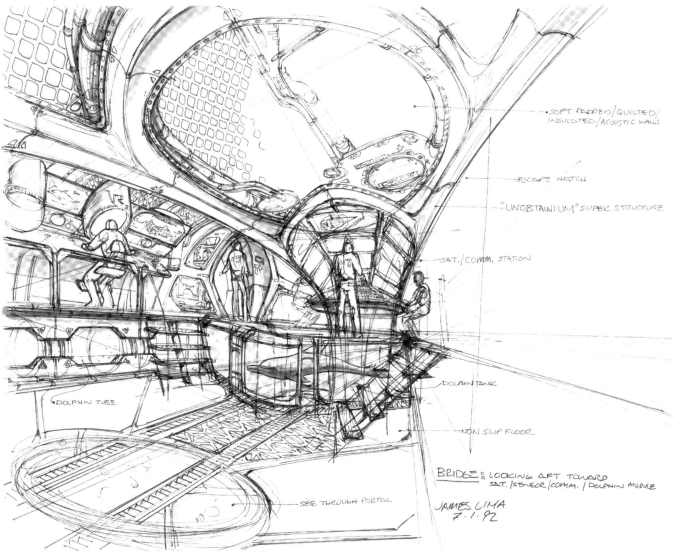

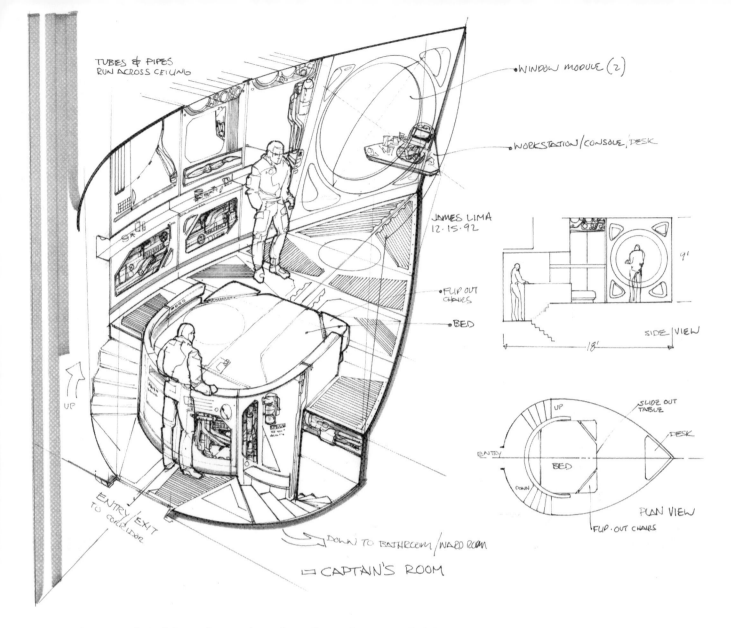

TUBES & PIPES RUN ACROSS CEILING

WINDOW MODULE (2)

WORKSTATION/CONSOLE, DESK

JAMES LIMA
12·15·92

FLIP OUT CHAIRS

BED

UP

ENTRY/EXIT TO CORRIDOR

DOWN TO BATHROOM/WARD ROOM

CAPTAIN'S ROOM

SIDE VIEW

9'

18'

UP

SLIDE OUT TABLE

DESK

ENTRY

BED

DOWN

PLAN VIEW

FLIP-OUT CHAIRS

someone to snap a shot of themselves as they edge – discreetly – into viewfinder range with the famous Captain James T. Kirk.

△ △ △ △ △ △

While they're setting up the next shot, the second A.D., beaming, whispers in a visitor's ear: "I just got off the phone with Kenny's wife," he says. "He got an ASC nomination. Only you and the A.D.s know."

The new year in Hollywood brings the start of the annual awards season, and Kenneth Zunder, the show's director of photography, has just received a nomination from his peers, the American Society of Cinematographers, for his work on the *seaQuest* pilot.

The D.P.'s incredulous: "For the pilot? Are you serious?"

"There'll be no dealin' with him now, boys," declares the second A.D., announcing the news to the entire crew. Applause and exclamations mix with the usual foxhole humour:

"Awright!"

"Hey, man, that's cool."

"Did you say the ASC award? We all knew he was gonna get one a' those."

"Speech! Speech!"

"Drinks for everyone!"

"Does this mean we get more money?"

But there's little time to joke – or to bask – when there are still more scenes to shoot. D.P. Zunder doesn't like the available camera angle for the next engine-room shot. He eyes a large octagonal tank labelled *Recirc H3*, giving the large prop a cursory tap. "This is gonna have to fly," he says, which in the jargon means no less than that the stagehands are going to have to move it out of the shot.

Dismay is written all over the nearest stagehand's face when he hears this, but "Which way, sir?" is all he says.

The Set Designer

The new engine-room set, constructed partly from the MagLev set, has been a "nightmare set because of the earthquake", Vaughn Edwards, the show's current production designer, says laconically in a soft British accent. "It started off on stage four, then we had to move it because stage four was condemned. We had to scramble to get it ready in time."

It was stages, rather than the sets themselves, that suffered from quake damage, he adds. "Two of the stages we worked on

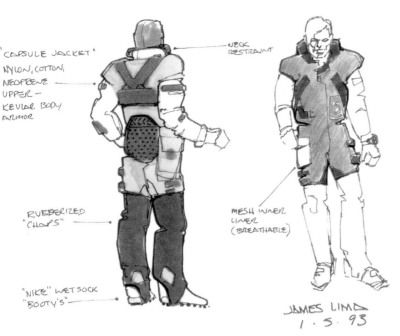

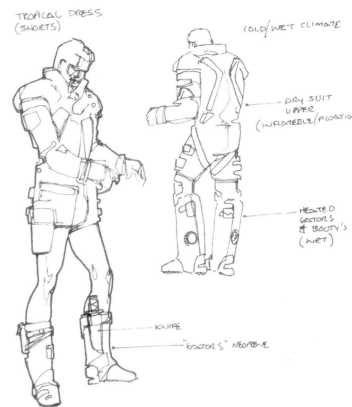

"CAPSULE JACKET"
NYLON, COTTON,
NEOPRENE
UPPER –
KEVLAR BODY
ARMOR

NECK
RESTRAINT

RUBBERIZED
"CHAPS"

MESH INNER
LINER
(BREATHABLE)

"NIKE" WET SOCK
"BOOTY'S"

JAMES LIMA
1 . 5 . 93

TROPICAL DRESS
(SHORTS)

COLD/WET CLIMATE

DRY SUIT
UPPER
(INFLATEABLE/FLOATION)

HEATED
GATORS
& BOOTY'S
(WET)

KNIFE

"GATORS" NEOPRENE

the lot, we had to move sets off of and on to other stages." Like many of the new writer/producers on board, he's a veteran of the much-admired but little seen *Tribeca,* an anthology series that had a brief run on the Fox network.

And while he's on set to deal with any problems that may arise, he's already thinking two episodes ahead, about the three to five sets – per average episode – he'll need to design and construct.

The engine-room set itself took "ten or twelve days" to build and it's fashioned from "sort of basic set-construction wood", he says. "Also there is a lot of moulded plexiglass in it that's made to resemble metal."

Asked to sum up the style of the show, he says "you might call it organic high-tech. The shapes are all very organic; they're based on shapes in nature, and streamlined shapes inspired by dolphins and whales and that kind of thing. But at the same time, it is a future world; it's an extremely scientific and technical design at the same time."

The Costumer

Robin Wright consults her deck of key-punched colour Polaroids hanging on a keyring attached to the belt loop of her jeans.

"This is how I keep up with who's wearing what," she says, fanning through the deck.

She is the self-described "female set costumer", and her job is to "make sure everyone's wearing the right clothes, because they never shoot in sequence. So, I just keep up with what everyone's wearing – [and make certain] they're wearing it properly [and are in] the right [costume] change for the right scene."

SeaQuest is her first TV series, and it's an easy one to work. "From my end of it, there's not tons of characters, there's not tons of extras."

Her Polaroid snaps are of the actors in the costume being worn for this day's scenes. There is, for example, a from-the-neck-down shot of Scheider in the casual khaki UEO uniform he wears in the bridge and the engine scenes. "Just to save on

pictures and not to hassle the actors too much, I don't keep taking pictures," she says. "This is what he's wearing; this is a good picture for all the times he wears this one outfit."

There's also a similarly truncated snapshot of Jonathan Brandis wearing one of his Lucas Wolenczak get-ups. The photo "shows you that his shirt's open, it's not buttoned, none of his sleeves are pulled up. You've gotta make sure some of the white around his neck is showing."

On the back of the Polaroid, Wright has neatly written all the particulars: "Baseball shirt, open, Twelve West, which is a logo on the shirt ... It's green and blue. A two-button, long-sleeve pullover shirt, untucked. A white, crew neck, short-sleeved tee shirt, untucked, and it's also hanging out. Khaki baggy pants. Black Reebok sneakers, black socks."

Outfits get mixed-and-matched from episode to episode, so Brandis may turn up in a later episode in the same shirts, with, say, a black turtleneck and black pants. It's all those uniforms, really, that make the show so simple, Costumer Wright, a self-described former punk rocker from Texas, concludes. "Uniform shows are very simple."

The Kid and the Camera

It's the big third-act-ending confrontation scene – Bridger and Tezlof facing off in the engine room – and Jonathan Brandis, who isn't in the scene, who, in fact, is finished for the day, comes loping in just to check it out, poking his head around the engine-room door, with its ENGINE ROOM – RESTRICTED ACCESS – SECURITY CLEARANCE REQ'D sign, to watch the two heavyweights rehearsing.

After a few minutes of intent observation, Brandis hops up into the camera operator's unoccupied seat, peering into the viewfinder of the Panaflex, adjusting it up and down, while an accommodating stagehand pushes the camera back and forth along its dolly track.

"I came down looking for food, actually," the young actor explains later in a whisper, after he's hopped off the camera seat. "Every once in a while you get a camera and a dolly track, which is very unlikely, because they usually clean it up real fast. I do it every chance I get."

"You getting into it?" he's asked.

"Yeah," says Brandis. "It's such a complicated piece of machinery."

Instinctively, the visitor wants to test him. "What's that gun for?" he asks, pointing to a gun-shaped device attached to the business end of the Panavision camera.

"It's for the zoom," Brandis replies immediately [and correctly]. "What they have on here is a five-to-one zoom lens. That gun enables you to zoom in fast or slow."

"Are you down here to see Shatner and Scheider?"

"Yes, I am. I only did one scene with him, and this is the first time he's worked in about four days. Yeah, he's terrific. The two of them together are somethin'."

"Have you learned anything watching Shatner, or haven't you seen him enough to make a judgement?"

"What amazes me is the infamous voice," Brandis replies, "which you've always heard in imitations and this and that. I hope I get a chance to ask about some of the stuff he's done, the classic stuff, not so much *Star Trek*, but *The Twilight Zone* episodes that he did. I'm a big fan of those."

"Whadya gonna ask him?"

"I'm probably gonna ask him what his favourite one was, 'cause he's done three or four of 'em. I know Rod Serling really liked him."

△ △ △ △ △

"It's called two units on the same stage," Director Parsons says, hurrying from the engine-room set, where the Recirc H3 prop is being pulled at and hammered on and generally gotten ready to fly out of A-camera's way, to another area of the huge stage and another set: an elevated length of catwalk inside a cutway tunnel, just then being lighted, where B-camera has been moved.

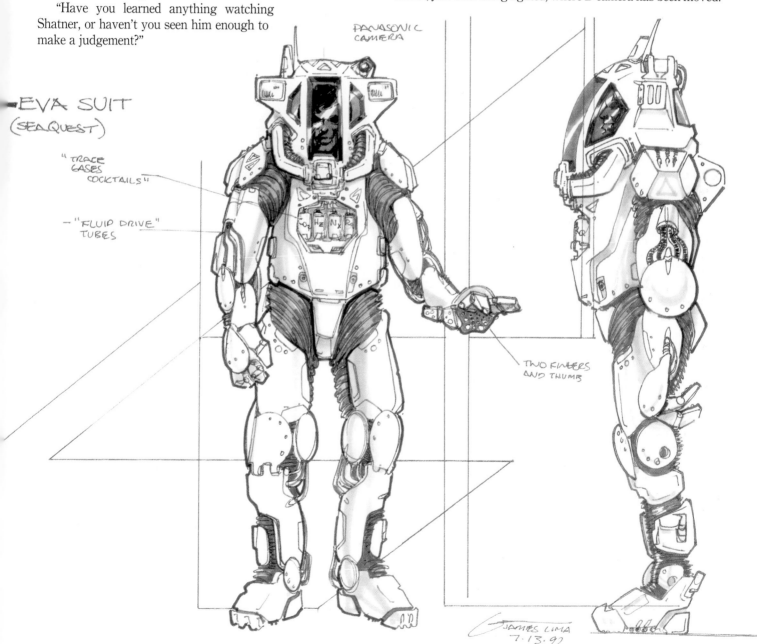

EVA SUIT
(SEAQUEST)

PANASONIC CAMERA

"TRACE GASES COCKTAILS"

- "FLUID DRIVE" TUBES

TWO FINGERS AND THUMB

JAMES LIMA 7.13.92

On *seaQuest,* says one veteran, it's not unusual to do forty to sixty "set-ups" per day, with twenty to thirty minutes required just to light each one.

△ △ △ △ △ △

"I'll take a turkey burger on an English muffin," says William Shatner, who's waiting for the next set-up, to the craft services man, and a visitor, overhearing, can't help wondering if there's a replicator hidden somewhere.

But Shatner, who directly strides away, seems confident that his order will be filled.

In Hollywood, above a certain level of fame or clout, you really do get a chair with your name on it, and this show is no exception. So, in addition to the chairs with the names of all the regulars, and the chairs with the names of the D.P. and the director, there is of course the guest star's chair. And it is to this – at the centre of the other, unoccupied chairs – that Shatner repairs to await his burger. Momentarily sitting alone, amidst the pounding noise and swirling bustle of the on-the-clock production crew, the famous actor presents a strangely poignant sight. But before the visitor can go over and engage him in conversation, the craft services man – as if beamed in from nowhere – appears, turkey burger on a muffin proudly displayed on the plate in hand.

Shatner balances the plate on his knees, but, just as he carefully lifts the burger two-handed, rehearsal is called. He wolfs down one bite only before, reluctantly, handing the food over to a second A.D., who politely, but firmly, heads him in the direction of the engine-room set.

△ △ △ △ △ △

Slurping down coffee from a styrofoam cup as he peers through the Panavision viewfinder, the D.P. is blocking out the shot, as Milos Tezlof walks slowly and deliberately toward Captain Bridger and Commander Ford.

Tezlof
I vant your vocorder and the dolphin. I vant to heal my son.

"And that's going to be the cut," the director says, meaning the end of the third act, but the tense confrontation scene resumes as well, after the commercial break, to begin the episode's fourth and final act. Shatner asks quietly if they can rehearse the scene in its entirety, as if there were no break.

"Of course," says the director, and they begin it again.

Shatner, as seems to be his habit in rehearsal, practically whispers the words, turning back to the script supervisor after the first few lines.

"'Heal', is it?" She consults the big book. "Make my son whole," she reads from the latest revision. Then she notices that the actor is wearing a wrist watch, which, for reasons of continuity, she askes him to remove. A normally hardbitten crew member, who couldn't look more like an adoring Trekker if he was wearing full Klingon make-up, eagerly offers to hold Captain Kirk's twentieth-century timepiece, but Shatner demurs, pocketing it himself instead. He runs through the lines

again, advancing on Scheider, who, like the very best, doesn't so much act as he does re-act with a silent eloquence.

Tezlof
I vant the dolphin and the vocorder. I vant to make my son whole.

They run through it yet again. Each time, despite off-stage coughing, hammering and other distracting clatter, Shatner's distinctive voice grows stronger, his delivery becomes more dramatic, more impassioned: his Tezlof is a man on the edge of an abyss, fighting to save his only son.

Bridger
What do you want?

Tezlof
I have a solution for you. I will give up my claims on my country. In return you will give me your dolphin and vocorder. And safe passage from this boat.

Bridger
(a beat)
I can't do that.

After the third walk-through, he turns back again to the script supervisor.

"Did I 'go up'?" Shatner wants to know.

She shakes her head, hugging the big book to her chest. "'I will *give* up,'" she quotes. "That was it." He nods solemnly, filing it away for when the camera starts to roll.

"All right, this will be picture! Picture's up!"

"Ninety-eight baker!"

"A bell and a red!"

"*Rrrriiing!*"

"Let's roll 'em!"

"Rolling!"

"Speed!"

"Very quiet."

"Settle!"

"And ... *Action!*"

When the shooting starts, director, D.P. and script supervisor are all gathered around the small black-and-white monitor to watch the shot Zunder has painstakingly constructed. This is what they see:

An Extreme Close-Up – Shatner in profile. As he begins his speech – "I have a solution for you" – the camera pulls back to an over-the-shoulder full shot of Scheider at the far end of the engine room, watching warily as Shatner approaches. As Bridger says, "I can't do that," the camera pushes in to a medium two shot, Scheider and Don Franklin behind him, then it pans with Shatner as he turns, again in profile, to the curved engine-room wall, all lights and dials. As he speaks, the camera pulls back again: a three shot, Scheider re-acting with a quick glance at Franklin, and ...

Rrrumble ...

"Cut!"

This time it's not an aftershock. A heavy truck has roared by outside, ruining the take. "Soundstages," mutters the D.P., shaking his head in disbelief, "you can hear every sound." While the camera is reloaded and moved back to its first position, he explains the scene's "unifying theme" to a visitor:

"It's not necessarily something that's in the set," he says. The actors on *seaQuest* are often lighted from both above and below, with D.P. Zunder taking advantage of the authentically grated submarine "floor" on the various sets to position lights under the action. This time, these lights cast up a cross-hatching that's seen only behind the good guy – Scheider – while throwing an eerie lighting net, a "harsh pattern" suggestive of prison bars, over the bad guy – Shatner – as he walks. Of such small details are ASC nominations made.

"And ... Rolling!"

"*Rolling!*"

"Mark."

"And ... *Action!*"

It's seven in the evening, eleven hours after the first set-up of the day. Once again, they take it from the top.

When they finally finish "Hide and Seek" the following afternoon, the crew immediately begins setting up for the next episode, and the shoot continues, despite yet another aftershock, until three in the morning.

It's TV and – until the respite known as hiatus at the end of the season – it never stops.

VIEWING DAILIES

David J. Burke, ever solicitous of a visitor's welfare, and his boon companion, Robert Engels, seem utterly at ease and ultra affable.

And why not? They are writer/producers by trade, and by title *seaQuest*'s executive producer and co-executive producer, respectively, the hot new hired guns on the production.

In TV it's a truism: the writer/producer is king. And, to quote Mel Brooks and other philosophers, it is good to be the king.

They, and their colleague Patrick Hasburgh, form a triumvirate, a team, brought aboard to oversee a much-remarked on "change in direction", a refocusing of the show [to fervent hallelujahs from Roy Scheider and Stephanie Beacham, in particular] on character-driven plotlines, rather than on whiz-bang gizmos and state-of-the-art special effects. Musing, Engels even suggests that "Darwin could be funny. Why couldn't he be? He could have another emotion other than godliness."

To an outsider it seems they're in an enviable position: if they pull it off – higher ratings, second-year renewal, favourable critical re-appraisals – they're heroes; if they don't, they're still The Pros, the guys Spielberg tapped with his *E.T.* magic finger, and they fought the good fight.

△ △ △ △ △ △

Straight off "Hide and Seek", they've begun shooting "The Good Death", an episode that will see Captain Bridger and his crew out of their twenty-first century submarine and among the timeless pre-Lenten celebrants of a Brazilian carnival. The basic idea for this episode came from Burke's seventeen-year-old son, and the writer-producer has on a third hat for this one; he's directing.

And today, while the crew breaks for lunch, he views dailies – that is, a tape of yesterday's raw footage – in the show's production trailer.

"The *seaQuest* has just disabled an old submarine that they've been told is smuggling emeralds out of South America, the Amazonian Confederation," he explains, as the tape silently begins to play – it's every take of a few particular scenes, "and they're about to board it to discover that in fact they're smuggling out children from the ghetto, impoverished children, and not emeralds.

"And they're doing it to protect the children from a dictatorial regime that, for the sake of [its] merchants, has been killing them. It goes on in Brazil to a limited degree now, that kind of behaviour, and it's a bit of a dark episode for us."

The episode was written by thirtysomething staff writer Hans Tobeason, from an original idea by Douglas Burke, who, in school, happened to be studying about the Civil War-era underground railroad that smuggled slaves out of the South, when he saw a news report on the vigilante killings of unwanted street children in Brazil.

"Once in a blue moon somebody gives you an idea that in the course of two or three sentences you can see the whole story," says Douglas' father, "and he'd given me one other idea that I'd used. I'd given him some money [for it] out of my own pocket." The idea, which Burke eventually wrote up, became the episode called "The Regulator". "He hadn't developed it as a story, but this time he came up with an idea that *really* worked; I saw the whole arc of it."

△ △ △ △ △ △

The on-screen kids, at least a dozen of them, are packed into the confining space of an ancient submarine that's foundering. They're solemn, scared. Bridger comes aboard to rescue them.

One at a time, says Bridger, trying to keep them calm while getting the frightened children up a ladder and out as fast as possible. *Take it easy! Follow me!*

Because it's raw footage, you can hear the kids getting off-screen direction, too: "Look at me, look at me, and: *Turn!* ... Okay, okay, towards the ladder. You're next ... *Cut it!*"

"I've never worked with this many kids before," says Burke, watching the several takes of a line of big-eyed street urchins, their hair closely cropped, all spin/turning at once toward the camera. "Steven has, I haven't."

"It was an incredible, chaotic scene yesterday," he adds, wonderingly, "and we wanted it to be chaotic, but we have children who are *supposed* to understand Portuguese – we're yelling at them in Portuguese – and they're not responding to the Portuguese because *they don't speak it!*" He laughs. "Huh-huh-huh!

"They're ten, twelve years old; they're not gonna be disciplined under any circumstances. Everybody on the set who had kids looked around and said, 'Yeah, why is there a surprise? They're ten years old, they're not listening.'"

The second A.D. brings in lunch – chicken, veggies and what appear to be institutional mashed potatoes – which Burke eats absent-mindedly while watching the "raw" on the monitor across the narrow trailer's single sparse room.

The crucial shot, he explains, is that tight shot of the children turning en masse at the off-camera cue and then rushing toward the ladder. "I'm all right," he says. "That turn I needed," he says quietly as another shot flies by. "They jam up, cut around, jam up ... Then the guy yells and they turn and look," he explains reciting the order of crucial connecting shots. "I'll be all right."

"I *think* I've got enough, I *think* I've got enough," he says again of the scene in which the kids turn together on cue. "Right here I'm looking for coverage."

"Coverage" is a term of art for footage that, well, *covers* you; it's something you can cut to and from, that can move you to another shot. As a visitor watches the brief sequence, it becomes more noticeable that the camera, jostling right along with the packed-in children, is on the move, too, darting in and out.

"I'm also looking at this because the A.D.'s been giving me a little grief about shooting this particular sequence all hand-held and rough," says Burke. "Nobody's done it before. Not that it's a big deal, but it's sorta not a style that *seaQuest* does, and it was appropriate for this, and Patrick Hasburgh really wanted to see some hand-held stuff. Steven's mentioned it once, and nobody really wanted to take responsibility.

"I mean, the other directors weren't comfortable with it," he adds. "Also, this scene lent itself to it."

Hand-held is something Burke is familiar with, and not just from his work on *Tribeca*. He took an unlikely route to episodic TV's creative heights, starting out toiling in lowly local TV news.

"That's where I learned to be lean and mean," he says of his time at Channel Five in New York City. "We produced an hour of news five nights a week, and a half-hour on the weekends. We were competing with stations that literally had three times the budget, and we did real well 'cause [the news director] would hire kids with no experience to support some seasoned reporters, and he took a chance that they were smart and aggressive enough to make up for the inexperience."

Now, though, not all the dailies Burke is looking for are on the tape. "We had some trouble in the lab," he says. "It's not the whole set of dailies ... but *it's* in here."

Burke puts down his knife and fork. "I'm a little bit relieved. I've got one problem in dailies that I can't do anything about, which is my fault. I'll just have to make it work." A particular child's acting moment is weak, his dialogue reading unconvincing. "I'll have music and effects [to] carry the moment. And it's not so bad that I can't live with it."

Living With It just might be emblematic of Burke's initial difficulties after coming aboard *seaQuest DSV*. "It was not a show that I either created or was in at the ground floor on," he says directly. "So I came in and there were a myriad of problems that were not mine, that were the result of the best intentions of decent people, but it was a problem and I had to come in and deal with it in a polite manner, trying to get things to settle down and jell, without, you know, throwing the baby out with the bathwater.

"And that was the hardest thing for me, because there are a lot of problems in evidence that could've been dealt with with a machete that, you know, [I] basically used a butter knife on."

Asked to summarise those problems, Burke ticks them off without hesitation: "It was inexperience, people in certain key positions; it was the lack of viewpoint on the show by people who were actually running it, in terms of agreement; there was an inability to communicate with Roy, who's the star. It is really *essential* that the executive producer and the star get along with each other and communicate."

Roy Scheider is a pro, Burke's visitor suggests. A *proper* actor, as Stephanie Beacham put's it. "He is. He's a pro. He is almost courtly in his manners and charm. He's a sweetheart. When he get's upset, it's only because he want's it better. Now, he doesn't want to be told, 'Here it is, do it.' And there was kind of a lot of that going on.

"Particularly a show like this, Roy is the anchor to it, and he needed somebody who likes working with actors. I like working with actors," Burke says. "So that part of it is great, and working with the crew is great, and working now with Hasburgh and Bob Engels is terrific. They're solid, seasoned guys; they're trying to make a show work that's very expensive by the nature of the beast.

"It's all money spent on technology; I'm not carting it home, Spielberg's not carting it home. It's going into the show."

And to someone who's spent time on the *seaQuest* stages, it's obvious that money is in those spectacular sets. "It's on the set, it's not the screen as much as it should be. That's what we're trying to do is get it there. But the team is working well now."

And the best part of the gig, he says, is working with the actors and running the production ship. "I really love what I'm doing right now. I didn't write this script [of the episode he's currently directing], but I supervised its writing and did a lot of the re-writing. I *love* coming in and directing and working with the cast and the crew. I *love* doin' that."

Ironically, being on a series is kind of like being on a submarine, a visitor suggests. "Well, it must be, because – if it's gonna – you have to have an *esprit de corps* and a tight working environment."

Can you maintain a life outside the demanding pace of the show?

"My past experiences, with *Crime Story, Miami Vice, Wise Guy* and *Tribeca* – all that was New York, Chicago, Vancouver and Miami – this is the first time I've been at home. My wife sees me every night; my son's on the set a lot ... maybe a little more than he ought to be, but I like it. I like that he's watching, paying attention."

And what the teenager likes most about the show, says Burke, is the "relationship between Lucas and Bridger. He has a personal relationship with both actors, but he separates pretty much what he watches ... And he likes the relationship between Darwin and Lucas and Bridger. He gripes to me, 'You gotta see more of Ford.'

"Beyond that, he's become pals with some of the younger actors, so he becomes their lobbyist sometimes – You know, 'Ted's not workin' enough, Dad' or 'Why don't we see more of Marco?'"

Burke himself has now worked with some of the most high-profile and high-powered writer/producer/directors around – from Michael Mann [*Miami Vice*] to Steven Cannell [*Wise Guy*] to Steven Spielberg.

"Steven Spielberg and Steven Cannell are masterful at their own craft in ways that other people aren't," says Burke. "They're also very charming, articulate men, who have a *great deal* of respect in public for other human beings. They should,

in some ways, be role models for behaviour among adults in public environments.

"Michael's much more aggressive and a smart-ass, and I'm more like Michael in a lot of ways. Stylistically, Michael is style over substance in a lot of ways, style *is* substance. And my experience with Steven is a little limited, because, you know, he's a guy on an imperial schedule.

"He's completely available to me, he's in there but it's like" – he snaps his fingers – "boom, boom, boom. Also, I've never met anyone who knows as much as he does about film, whether it's film on television or film in the movies. He knows everything.

"Spielberg's a writer to me, I think of him as a writer ... a storyteller ... He really knows how to tell a story."

Now that he's taken the helm of the *seaQuest,* what does he envision doing differently? "I wanna get out of the ship and get into the water with our characters, into the ocean, diving, researching and being up on land more. The submarine finally is a vessel for getting you places and doing science and providing protection and flying the flag, but I wanna connect with the world twenty-five years from now. That we haven't been able to do this year in a big way. All the effort was put originally into the submarine.

"If we can get through this season, we can start next season as really a happy group of people, and the dissension won't exist anymore. It will be discussion."

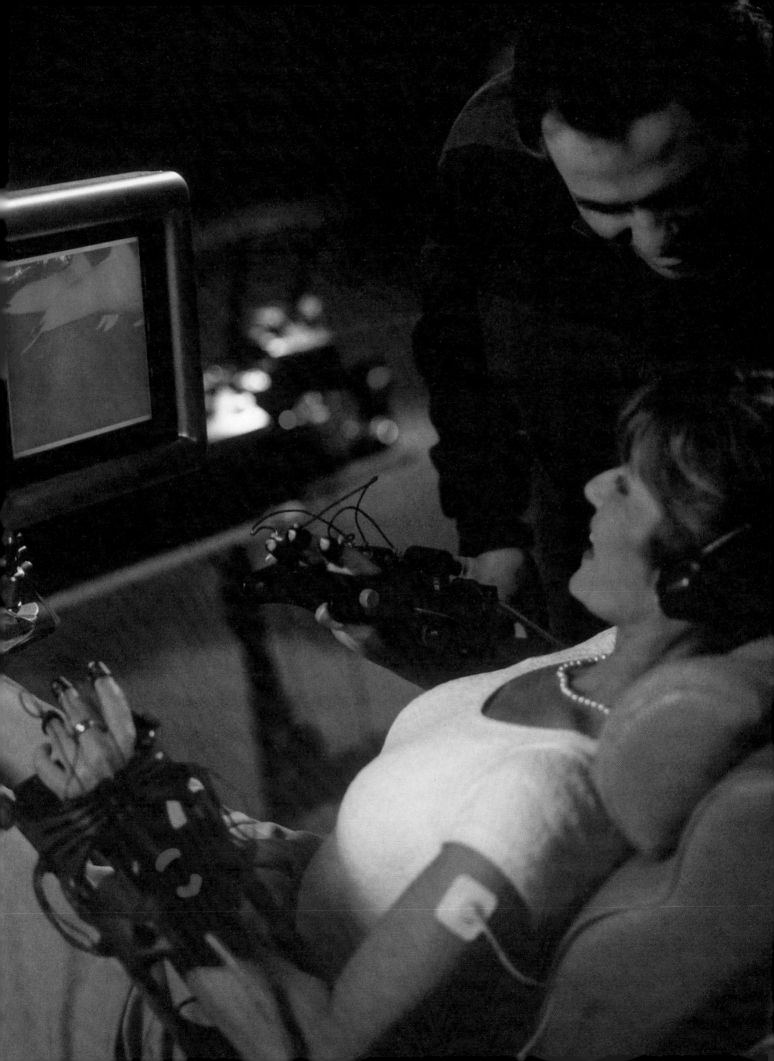

The trailer door flies open and in comes the co-executive producer, Robert Engels, all crinkly smiles and shaggy hair. He's all decked in casual earth-tone silks and is holding a big, unlit cigar.

"Hey, Bob," Burke calls out happily. "I hired him as an actor," Burke continues, pointing across the room with his fork, as Engels, chuckling, settles sprawling into a chair on the other side of the narrow room. "And he's known in town as a writer-producer, and he's *spectacular*. And he's a recurring character!" Burke adds, his voice rising to meet Engels' laughs.

"Okay, maybe he's not John Barrymore," Burke continues, warming to the subject, as Engels shakes his head, demurring with stagey, mock modesty: "No, no."

But, Burke says, "It's great fun to have a friend and co-worker who can do something else on the show."

"Hah!" says Engels, when Burke is asked if the co-executive producer can take direction.

"Yeah, he does actually."

"Yes, I do," Engels interjects, "but I have a real dirty mind."

"His agent thinks he's like Tom Cruise now, but ..."

"Hah!"

"He created this character who in a lot of ways is Roy's favourite other male adult to relate to, which is Malcolm Landsdowne, and it's very cool, because now he can write and act in an episode ... It keeps energy going."

"Yeah," Engels agrees, "and keeps the crew fresh. Don'tcha think?"

"Yeah ... He wrote himself a little love scene with Stephanie."

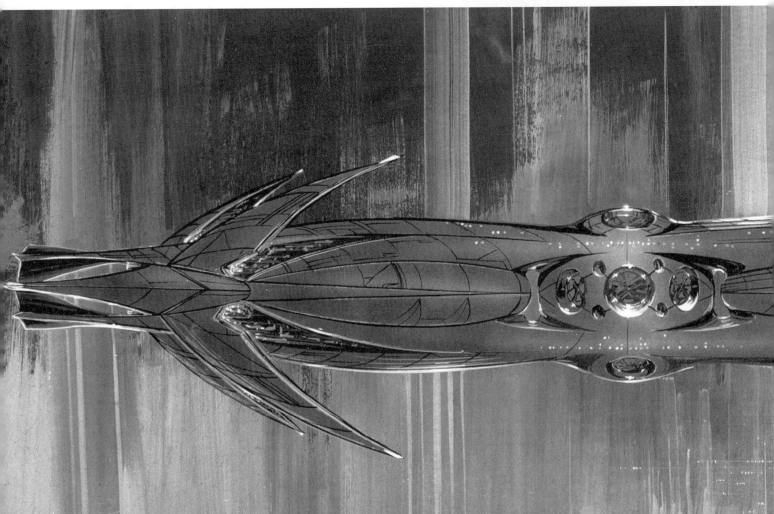

"Ho! Ho!"

"Yeah!"

"It was arrived at mutually."

"Ah-hah?"

"But, ah."

Clearly, these are two men who understand each other. His demurrals notwithstanding, it turns out Bob Engels *has* acted in the past, on soaps. "It's hard to not adjust your lines," he says.

All the while, the dailies continue to run: now, scenes of poor, but colourfully costumed, Brazilians living in *favelas* [the local term for ghettoes] flash by; mingling among them, a nearly shirtless Don Franklin as Commander Ford and a beautiful brown-skinned woman, who catches the producers' attention again.

"The girl's spectacular to look at," says Engels.

"And she's a really good actress."

"There were more male production assistants that found a reason to be around Les's office during auditions."

"[The word] spread like sort of a secret message."

"The poor girls [auditioning] ... like they didn't catch on immediately ... I'm gonna have a crane shot here."

"The Russians had an experiment where they could bring their wives [on sub missions]," says Engels, musing, "right before perestroika and all that ... The Russians let their hair grow and let their beards grow [on missions]."

Hmmm, you can hear Burke thinking and he says, "That would be interesting."

"Yeah, I think that's not a bad idea," Engels replies mildly, enquiring about the crane shot.

"God, I shot a lot of film," says Burke, as the dailies silently flash by.

"Who's gonna tell you not to?" Engels shoots back.

"That *is* pleasant."

"I WANT THE CRANE!" cries Engels, in full mock tantrum.

"Awright awright awright."

"I'M NOT GONNA MOVE TILL I GET MY CRANE!"

Again, with no forewarning, the trailer door opens suddenly. It's Ken Zunder, the D.P., and John Kretchmer, the first A.D., peering in. "It's comin' up soon," says Zunder matter-of-factly. "It was B-camera."

"Fifteen minutes," Kretchmer says, "then we'll do a rehearsal with the troops."

Suddenly, it's sound up on the dailies: Brazilian Carnival drums. Pan across a *favela* – extras crossing, doing bits of business – then up and across a roof to find the beautiful young actress ...

"That's my crane shot ... That's it, Bob."

"Very cool, very cool ... That's a beautiful woman."

"No pain casting those roles."

The crane shot took three takes, Burke recalls. "Actually we got it pretty quick ... It does show what the *favela* is gonna be like."

"With the music it'll be cool, and the girl on the roof is a surprise."

"A little cheesecake for the guys at NBC. We got Ford ... shirtless, so I got some beefcake. And ten-year-old boys. So everybody's covered. We've got all the bases covered."

THE FUTURE HISTORY OF THE WORLD

It'll come as no surprise to its cultural critics, but the bibles found throughout Hollywood are *not* necessarily the amening kind.

Rather, "bible" is a show business term-of-art referring to the guidelines compiled for a TV series. In a series bible, the testaments are synopses of story lines, descriptions of recurring characters; the do's and don'ts for new writers pitching a prospective idea or writing a show.

The original *seaQuest* bible was assembled by writer Rockne S. O'Bannon long before the series was first aired. You'll find descriptions of characters who never actually made the ultimate cut like "journalist/educator" Liana Hays, an on-board correspondent for EarthNet, the twenty-first century's global news network.

Important to any bible – and most good series – is "back-story" (or we could call it the Old Testament), which is the story that *precedes* the plotline airing week-to-week on the series. Often it also involves the pre-series history of the recurring characters. Backstory might tell you how young Lucas came to be aboard the *seaQuest* or how Nathan Bridger met his wife, for example. This information is invaluable to both the writer who derives stories out of the characters, as well as for the actor trying to give life to the creation.

The future history of the world up to the year twenty-eight-een – mixing backstory with fact-based science fiction, is a significant feature of that original *seaQuest* bible, and it follows in its entirety.

1990

▲ Berlin Wall falls.

1991

▲ USSR disintegrates.
▲ Seaman 1st Class Nathan Hale Bridger, his third year in the Navy, serves aboard the USS *Aurora* in the Gulf War.

1992

▲ World Ecology Summit convenes in Rio showing first serious signs of mankind's interest in earth's survival.
▲ At same time, CIS/USA (Yeltsin/Bush) begin far-reaching military disarmament.
▲ Seaman Bridger embarks on naval officer training at Annapolis.

1996

▲ Need for global nuclear warfare capability among super-powers all but gone.
▲ Worldwide search for answers to ecological survival continues.
▲ Realisation begins to dawn that world's oceans could be saving grace environment for earth ... yielding seemingly limitless new sources of food, fuel, living space, etc.

▲ Programmes are begun to study feasibility of deep-sea exploration and utilisation.
▲ Ensign Bridger applies for service in the Submarine Corps.

1999

▲ Technologies are rapidly developing which make the seas a much less foreboding environment. Large-scale desalination of sea water, deep-sea oil drilling, ore mining, "farming", even colonisation – are suddenly very possible.
▲ Nations earmark large portions of their former military budgets toward swift development of these technologies.
▲ R&D resources previously directed toward outer space exploration are now aimed toward planet's oceans.
▲ Scientific and environmental communities pleased by these advances, also warn governments to proceed cautiously.
▲ Lt. Commander Bridger begins service as Exec Officer aboard the submarine, USS *Newport*.

2001

▲ "Surfscrapers" – buildings constructed half below water, half above – begin to appear off the shores of several major coastal cities.

▲ Sub-surface freighters begin service. (By travelling just beneath the surface, these ships are not affected by the vagaries of terrestrial weather, rough seas, etc., allowing safer, faster, more reliable passage.) Early sub-surface shipping lanes are established.

▲ First deep-ocean "environments" are established by various individual nations; some are oil drilling rigs, some are mining facilities, some are rudimentary "farms".

▲ The sea is living up to its potential: yielding fresh water, food, fuels, precious minerals, etc.

▲ Because of the expense of developing the necessary technologies, several smaller nations band together to form economic confederations similar to the European Common Market, so as not to be left behind.

2002

▲ More undersea "environments" are established. Because of the richness of resources at these chosen sites, most nations ignore the age-old rules of the open sea (the 200-mile limit), and begin staking claims to parcels of the ocean floor – and the regions of water above them.

▲ More countries band together into confederations to better expand their "ownership" of undersea property, and to strengthen their resistance to invaders.

▲ Environmentalists warn that the sea's resources are being exploited too rapidly. But the economic stakes are too high now; most nations and confederations ignore these warnings.

▲ Nathan Bridger attains the rank of Captain, and is given command of the submarine, USS *Aegis*.

2004

▲ Well-financed industrialists, independent of any nation or confederation, begin their own unregulated exploitation of the sea.

▲ Drug runners and other contraband traders begin using sub-surface vessels for their smuggling (rendering them totally undetectable to satellites, surface ships and planes, etc.).

▲ The United States joins with other countries to form the North Pacific Confederation.

▲ World tension mounts as ocean territoriality escalates.

2006

▲ The United Nations dissolves ... unable to cope with the power of these newly formed confederations and the rapidly rising antagonism among them.

▲ The USS *Aegis*, under the command of Capt. Bridger, effects the rescue of a downed mid-Atlantic confederation sub-surface passenger liner. Because the *Aegis* enters mid-Atlantic territory to perform the rescue, it is fired upon by mid-Atlantic forces. Later, although privately commended for their daring act of heroism, Bridger and the *Aegis* are officially censured by the North Pacific Confederation for aiding and abetting a foreign vessel in hostile waters.

▲ The eight world confederations begins to re-arm themselves using twenty-first-century technology.

2007

▲ Project *seaQuest* begins. The North Pacific Confederation commences design of the ultimate seagoing war vessel. The *seaQuest* (DSV 4600) will be the largest, fastest, deadliest machine ever to roam the seven seas. The maximum security project is placed under the direct supervision of Capt. Nathan Bridger.

2008

▲ Project *seaQuest* continues.
▲ Oceanic territoriality continues to escalate among the confederations. Deep-sea piracy and environmental rape of the oceans increase unabated.

2010

▲ Project *seaQuest* is nearing completion.
▲ An oceanic border dispute erupts in the Arctic. A North Pacific Confederation explorer ship is sunk by enemy fire. Capt. Bridger's only son is on board.
▲ Bridger finally sees the full evil potential of the ship he is building, and the insane path of self-destruction the world is on. He resigns from the project – and from the Navy.
▲ He and his wife travel to the remote Galapagos Islands and begin an ascetic life of marine research.

2013

▲ The *seaQuest* is commissioned, and sails under the command of Captain Marilyn Stark.

2015

▲ The *seaQuest* roams the seas, a foreboding presence, fully armed and ready to fight. She is a symbol of the constant threat of world war and world destruction. Other confederations rush to design their own versions of this superb sub.
▲ In the Galapagos, Capt. Bridger's wife contracts a respiratory disease and does not recover. Bridger vows to continue his research alone.

2017

▲ The Livingston Trench Incident occurs. Warrior submersibles from five federations converge on the Livingston Trench, each determined to protect their confederation's claim to this undersea region. The *seaQuest* is one of the five. Warheads are armed, world war seems inevitable.

The present ...
2018

▲ After eight years of remote island research, Capt. Bridger is lured back to civilisation by his lifelong friend, Admiral Tarr.

▲ The Livingston Trench incident did not lead to war. It lead instead to the formation of the United Earth/Oceans Organisation – a new United Nations, dedicated to creating and maintaining a new and lasting world peace. All eight confederations have warily signed on as member states – dissolving all undersea borders established over the past eighteen years.

▲ Beyond the re-established 200-mile limit, the oceans will be an "open frontier" once more. Confederations and industrialists will be free to maintain their existing undersea "environments", and to establish new ones – but the ocean floor and regions of water surrounding these environments will now be open territory.

▲ Also, the United Earth/Oceans Organisation is establishing guidelines for a safe, more ecologically responsible exploration and utilisation of the ocean's resources.

▲ It's a bold experiment, fraught with dangers as the whole of mankind attempts to pull back from the brink of world war, to establish this new world peace, and to launch into the twenty-first century working with the earth's ecology in a thoughtful, responsible way that it never has before.

▲ As an olive branch offering to this new era of hopeful co-operation, the North Pacific Federation bestows their flag-ship war vessel, the *SeaQuest,* upon the United Earth/Oceans Organisation. She is to sail under their new flag, with a multinational crew ... and to be refitted as a science vessel, now using all of her considerable cutting-edge technology in the exploration and discovery of deep-sea regions at yet unknown.

▲ And they want Bridger to return to active duty and assume command of her.

▲ Despite his cynicism that man will eventually find a way to either blow himself up or pollute himself out of existence, Bridger reluctantly agrees. And the *seaQuest,* under the command of Capt. Nathan Hale Bridger, sets sail on her new mission.

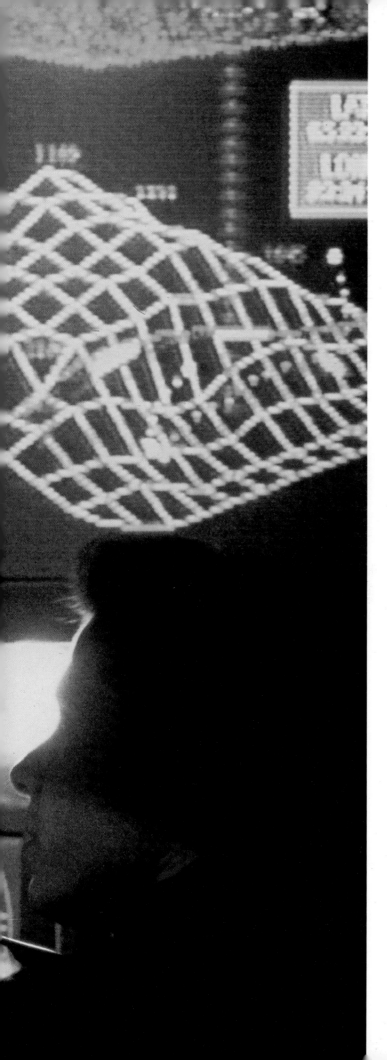

THE *SEAQUEST* ADVENTURES

Each week, the studio that distributes *seaQuest* and the network that airs it send out episode synopses to entertainment-reporters and editors in cities wherever the show airs.

These breathlessly written documents are intended to draw press interest for possible stories – "free media", as press agents and marketing experts call it – as well as to provide the necessary information for "loglines", those one sentence or less summaries of an episode plot that turn up each week in your local TV viewing guide.

Those *seaQuest DSV* synopses, usually seen only by industry insiders or Fourth Estate professionals, follow:

"To Be Or Not To Be" (premiére)

In the year 2018, mankind is moving closer toward utilising the full bounty of the earth; establishing small undersea farming, mining and manufacturing comunities; plumbing the depths with new technology and good old-fashioned human determination. But along with all this newfound potential comes the heightened reality of greed, opportunism and territoriality. It is also a time set in the future when a spectacular, highly advanced submarine explores the oceanic wonders – it is the *seaQuest DSV*.

In the première episode, Captain Marilyn Stark, commander of the 1000-foot-long Nor-Pac military submarine, *seaQuest DSV* (Deep Submergence Vehicle), arrives at the Livingston Trench, just as rival Confederations (economic and social unions of countries, peoples, and corporations) teeter on the verge of igniting a global conflict. Stark's reactions are surprisingly outside of military guidelines, and only the steady hand of Commander Jonathan Ford saves *seaQuest* from triggering the very clash it was sent to prevent. Captain Stark is relieved of duty due to mental instability.

And so it is that thirteen months later, Ford is in charge of the dry-docked *seaQuest* as she awaits her next mission. During the interim, as heated passions cooled into reason, the divergent Confederations formed a new worldwide body – the United Earth/Oceans Organisation (UEO) – to administer policy and adjudicate disputes. Indicative of the desire for lasting peace, Nor-Pac donated *seaQuest* to the UEO, allowing the greatest submergence vehicle ever built to serve the peace-

keeping and scientific needs of the whole planet. To service this noble plan, *seaQuest* has spent the last year being refitted to accommodate a large science contingent (actually outnumbering the military crew).

Heading up the scientific end of the operation is the fiery, dedicated Dr Kristin Westphalen, who often clashes with Commander Ford over their differing interpretations of *seaQuest*'s primary mission: the age-old battle between science and military.

Rounding out *seaQuest*'s bridge crew are Lt. Commander Katherine Hitchcock, the intense, driven Chief Engineer and second-in-command under Ford; Chief of Security Manilow Crocker, a crusty long-time Navy man who remembers "the old days" with fondness; Lieutenant O'Neill, the talented communications officer; and Sensor Chief Miguel Ortiz, the man in charge of *seaQuest*'s three revolutionary external probes called "Whiskers".

Only one final piece to the puzzle remains ... The new world order demands a new kind of captain. The dilemma for UEO Admiral William Noyce is to find someone who balances the requisite military acumen with a "feeling" for issues other than battle and weapons: A Renaissance man of the sea. With this in mind, there's only one place Noyce can logically turn: the designer, architect, and driving force behind the creation of *seaQuest* (though he never saw her finished), retired Captain Nathan Bridger. Unfortunately, Captain Bridger fled to a remote island with his wife, Carol, six years before, following the death of his son Robert (a junior naval officer). He made a promise to Carol that he would never have anything to do with the military again. Unfortunately, his idyllic life was shattered with the death of his beloved wife.

When we first meet him, Bridger is alone on his island, with his loyal dolphin – Darwin – with whom he has developed a rudimentary communication system involving hand signals. Reluctantly allowing himself to be convinced by Admiral Noyce, Bridger agrees to visit *seaQuest* "just to see how she turned out". Once aboard, however, Bridger discovers the true scope of Noyce's intentions. The *seaQuest* breaks from port and heads into open ocean with the furious Bridger trapped aboard. Further fuelling Bridger's anger, Noyce has secretly brought Darwin aboard, allowing him to swim through a series of access tubes spanning the boat – which Bridger actually designed in his original concept. However, Bridger's indignation is momentarily sidetracked when he discovers that in this environment, Darwin can understand human speech, and through the interpretive powers of *seaQuest*'s computers ...

THATCHED ROOF (WORN-IN)

PALMS

FLOWERS

SAND

SHRUBS

BRIDGERS HUT

JAMES LIMA 1.14.95

BLEACHED WOOD

actually speak! This revolutionary development in cetacean/human interaction is the brainchild of Lucas Wolenczak, the 16-year-old computer genius living onboard the *seaQuest*. In addition, Lucas is working on a project Bridger was beginning work on when he retired: a lifelike holographic representation of the ship's computer that can appear in the captain's quarters to "provide a sounding board in times of moral or ethical conflict".

Hoping to persuade Bridger to reconsider his retirement, Noyce has arranged for *seaQuest* to respond to an incident involving a renegade sub (not connected to any confederation; plying the seas for personal profit). Roaming the seas in command of the pirate submarine, brilliant but implacable in her Ahab-like thurst for revenge, is *seaQuest*'s former Captain ... Marilyn Stark. To lure her quarry into her net, Stark deliberately attacks a major undersea power station, knowing that *seaQuest* will speed to the rescue. Stark is eerily confident. Aware of Noyce's intentions from almost the beginning, Bridger resists taking the bait. However, something unexpected happens – the computerised weapons and defence systems shut down and refuse to respond when ordered to engage the rebel sub. The crisis quickens when the first torpedo from Stark's sub slams into the *seaQuest*'s hull. Quickly taking charge, Bridger gives orders to dive the ship into an ocean trench for safety until they can figure out what's going wrong. Stark's sub, unable to follow to the depths *seaQuest* can weather, breaks off combat and turns instead to attack another submerged colony not far away. Aboard *seaQuest,* Lucas finds the problem – an ingeniously designed virus planted deep inside the master computer programme some thirteen months earlier. A little more research gives Bridger the saboteur: Marilyn Stark, who just happened to be one of his pupils at the naval academy. The problem remains: any attempt to re-program and disarm the virus will trigger it to shut down all the ship's systems – including life support. Bridger draws on his knowledge of the *seaQuest*'s design to find a way around the computer and at least rig up the bare minimum of offensive weapons capability. They'll be able to shoot off one torpedo.

The hull repaired, *seaQuest* powers up and emerges from her hiding place to go on the attack. Swimming ahead, Darwin plants an electronic homing device on the hull of the rebel submarine. Stark, still overconfident, turns to deliver what she thinks will be the deathblow to *seaQuest*. But, to her surprise, she hears the

voice of Captain Bridger over the radio instructing her to surrender, followed by a single torpedo slamming into her own sub. *SeaQuest*'s probes follow her down to take survivors. Unfortunately, Marilyn Stark has escaped aboard a mini-sub.

Ultimately, Bridger faces the tormenting decision of how to reconcile his oath to Carol with the future that so resonantly calls him back to his proper place at the helm of *seaQuest*. He's not certain whether he will stay aboard, but a voice sounds over the intercom: "Captain to the bridge!" Bridger has to admit it – that means him. The crew of the *seaQuest* is complete, and her mission now begins in earnest.

The episode was written by Rockne S. O'Bannon and was directed by Irvin Kershner.

"The Devil's Window"

Two miles beneath the surface, *seaQuest* explores one of the ocean's truly remarkable phenomena: steaming hot hydrothermal vents play host to an underwater forest of giant tube worms and other forms of life where none was thought possible. Dr Raleigh Young wishes to cap the vent and exploit its incredible power. Young, a brash man of science, marches through his tours of discovery with the finesse of a bull, while Dr Westphalen questions – even fears – the Doctor's propensity for groping into the unknown.

In the meantime, Captain Bridger and Lt. O'Neill discover a mysterious aptitude for communicating with Darwin. But when his dolphin becomes deathly ill, Bridger is forced to choose between the mission at hand, and the life of one of his crew. As the mystery of Darwin's illness evades even Dr Westphalen, Bridger looks upworld, beyond traditional medicine, in order to find a cure.

The episode was written by David J. Burke and Hans Tobeason, and was directed by Les Landau.

"Treasures of the Mind"

While on an archaelogical mission in the Mediterranean Sea, Captain Bridger and his crew discover an annex of the great Library of Alexandria. The crew of *seaQuest* pulls magnificent ancient artifacts – statues, jewellery, exquisite bronze work, containers and clay tablets, from the ocean floor. Supposedly destroyed by both natural disasters and human plunder, the library has transcended probability. An air pocket has formed, protecting the contents of one of the rooms.

But when word of the discovery leaks from the *seaQuest*, Captain Bridger and his crew find themselves in the middle of an international incident. Many nations lay claim to the priceless artifacts, and send military forces to secure their recovery.

Despite Bridger's opposition, he is instructed by Admiral Noyce to mediate a Mid-East conference on the library. Aiding him in the mediation will be a UEO ESP team headed up by a Soviet immigrant (Torhan Bey). While none of the *seaQuest* crew is comfortable transporting people who can read their minds, Captain Bridger makes a special connection with the female member of the team (Lindsay Frost). In the meantime, Dr Westphalen makes a re-connection with an old colleague (Topol) on board to help with the excavation.

The episode was written by David Kemper and was directed by Bryan Spicer.

"Games"

Racing to the Antarctic polar ice cap, Captain Bridger and the *seaQuest* rescue a prison warden and his sole inmate – a brilliant but deranged scientist named Zellar, accused of mass murder and kept frozen in a cryogenic chamber. However, it is soon uncovered that the madman is impersonating the dead warden. Bridger, uneasy with Zellar aboard, locks him in the *seaQuest*'s brig. Diabolically, Zellar escapes and continues his killing spree, holding the submarine in a siege of terror.

Setting a laser beam trap for Bridger and security chief Crocker, Zellar is surprised by Ensign Darwin, the ship's dolphin, who comes to the rescue of his Captain. Zellar and Bridger then come together in a deadly match of wits as the madman demands that missiles are launched at Hawaii or he will unleash a killer toxin on the *seaQuest*.

The episode was written by David Venable and was directed by Joe Napolitano.

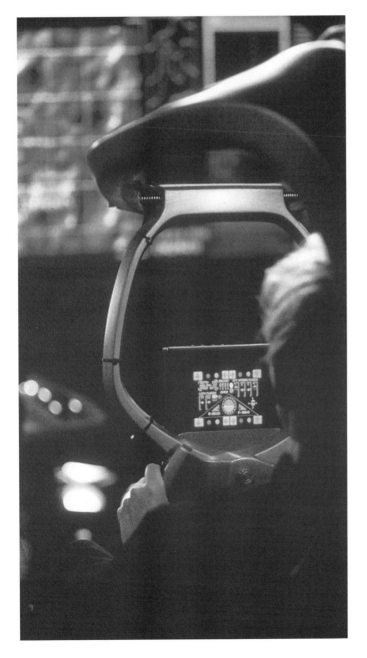

"Treasures of the Tonga Trench"

After Lt. Krieg brings back an underwater gem to the *seaQuest*, the prospect for fortune reveals hints of greed in some of the least likely members of the crew. Lt. Commander Hitchcock wonders why the entrepreneurial Lieutenant Krieg is less than eager to return to the deep murky depths for more. In the meantime, the crew of the *seaQuest* is administered comprehensive operating proficiency exams under the strict and unyielding gaze of Captain Jack Clayton. The visiting Captain's cut-throat manner challenges Captain Bridger's competitive spirit.

The episode was written by John J. Sakmar and Kerry Lenhard, and was directed by Les Sheldon.

"Brothers and Sisters"

Captain Bridger brings the *seaQuest* to a deserted munitions plant that must be entombed before structural weakening unleashes a deadly weapons explosion. Suddenly, their submarine is targeted. On closer inspection, Bridger makes a startling discovery – there are children in the plant! Commander Ford takes a launch crew to the plant but is unexpectedly held prisoner by the armed children headed by Zachary Thomas. The children believe their parents went for help and will return. One of the boys is quite ill and needs immediate medical treatment in the *seaQuest*'s hyperbaric chamber.

Ford is successful in getting him aboard the *seaQuest* but remains a hostage in the munitions depository. The ill boy is treated by Dr Westphalen, and the ship's young computer expert Lucas strikes up a friendship with the accompanying Cleo. She encourages Lucas to take them back to the plant because of Zachary. At the same time, Bridger makes another discovery – the children's parents are dead in the shuttle in which they sought help. He must convince Zachary and the children of this and escape the munitions plant before everyone dies in the growing underwater turbulence.

The episode was written by Art Monterastelli and was directed by Bill L. Norton.

"Give Me Liberté ..."

Captain Bridger fights the clock to help Commander Ford and other crew members who are contaminated with a deadly, secret virus after investigating the *Liberté,* a corporate-owned space station lost when it crashed in the sea years before, causing chemical danger.

In the *seaQuest* launch, Bridger and security chief Crocker race for the surface to find French scientist Dr Guy Peche, believed to possess knowledge of an antidote. Below on the *seaQuest*, Ford and the others remain in the ship's contamination chamber, their health rapidly deteriorating.

Bridger brings Dr Peche aboard the *seaQuest,* but he must also face down a fellow warrior submarine sent by the global company to blow up the *Liberté*. Lt. Commander Hitchcock launches battle counter-measures. Captain Bridger must board the *Liberté* and quickly solve the deadly peril affecting them or many will die.

The episode was written by John J. Sakmar and Kerry Lenhart, and was directed by Bill Norton.

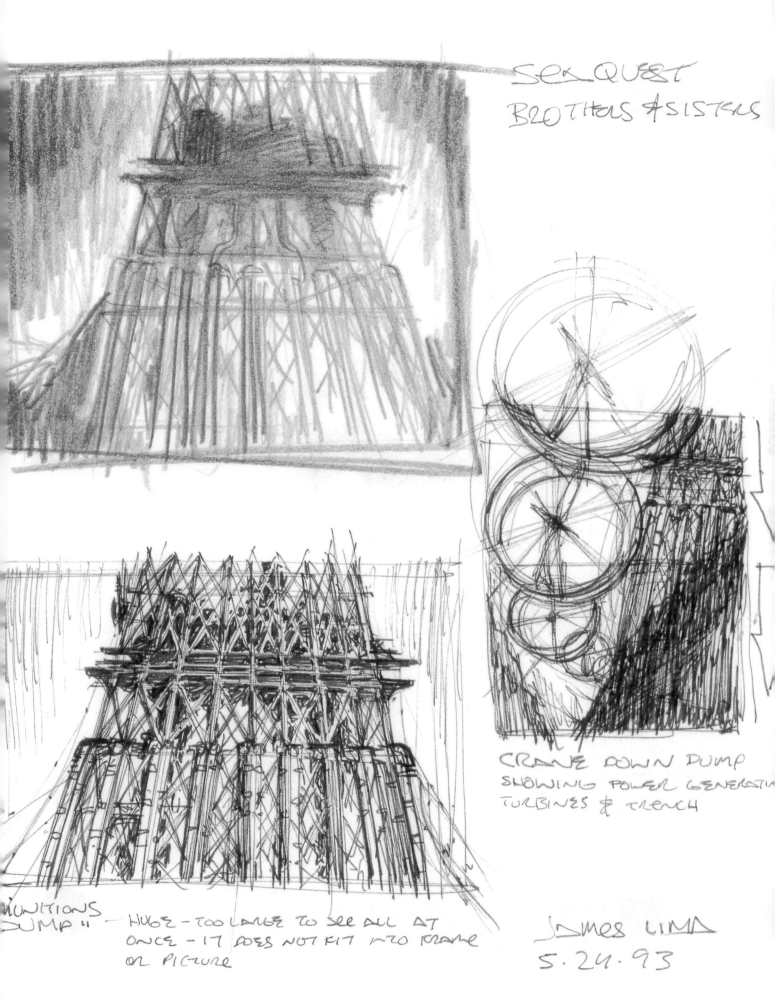

SEA QUEST
BROTHERS & SISTERS

CRANE DOWN DUMP
SHOWING POWER GENERATING
TURBINES & TRENCH

MUNITIONS
DUMP " — HUGE — TOO LARGE TO SEE ALL AT
ONCE — IT DOES NOT FIT INTO FRAME
OR PICTURE

JAMES LIMA
5.24.93

"Knight of Shadows"

The tone is set for an out of this world mystery/adventure when Captain Bridger is inexplicably summoned by Professor Martinson. When Bridger sets *seaQuest*'s course according to the hologram's instructions, he finds himself at the wreckage of the *King George*, a luxury liner which mysteriously sank one hundred years earlier.

When Captain Bridger and his crew go aboard to investigate, various clues to the ship's sinking fantastically reveal themselves. But to someone, the *seaQuest* crew are unwelcome guests, and some puzzles are better left unsolved.

Unable to explain the strange goings-on rationally, Bridger looks to Dr Levin's experience with the paranormal for additional insight. In the end though, it is some of the least likely crew members who help to unravel the mysteries behind the *King George*.

The episode was written by Melinda Snodgrass and was directed by Helaine Head.

138

"Bad Water"

Hurricane conditions threaten a downed French sightseeing submarine off the coast of Florida. With a dead pilot and all surface rescue vessels chased away by violent currents, *seaQuest* is their only hope for survival.

Double jeopardy ensues when a rescue launch carrying Krieg, Westphalen, Lucas and Ford runs into its own trouble, leaving the four crew members to battle the stormy conditions in a life boat. As a result, Captain Bridger is faced with the dilemma of prioritising between the lives of his crew and those of the vacationers. In the meantime, superstitious members of the crew can't help but think about the misfortune that this area, nicknamed the Bermuda Triangle, is best known for.

The episode was written by David Kemper and was directed by Bryan Spicer.

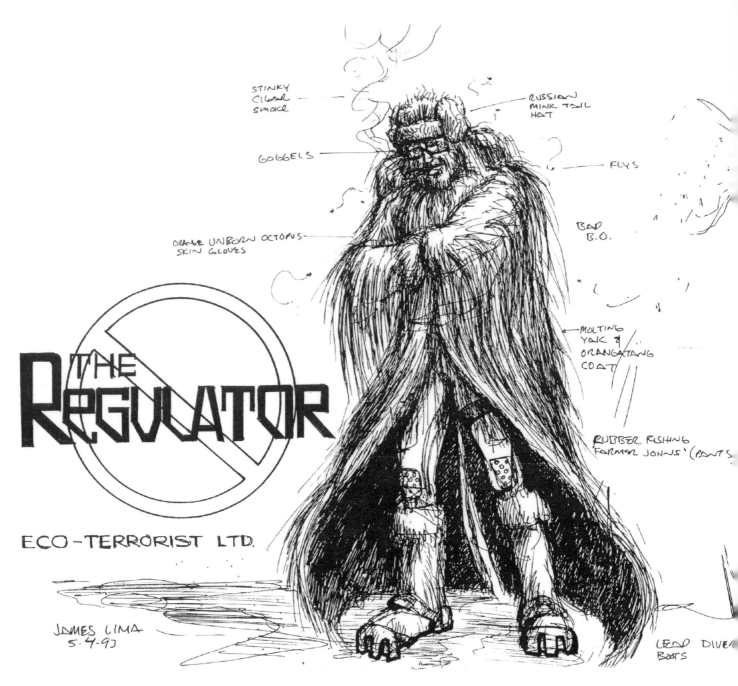

STINKY CIGAR SMOKE

GOGGELS

ORANGE UNBORN OCTOPUS SKIN GLOVES

RUSSIAN MINK TAIL HAT

FLYS

BAD B.O.

MOLTING YAK & ORANGATANG COAT

RUBBER FISHING FORMER JOHNS' (PANTS

LEAD DIVER BOOTS

THE REGULATOR

ECO-TERRORIST LTD.

JAMES LIMA 5.4.93

"The Regulator"

When the air conditioning breaks down in one of the sleeping quarters, tempers all over *seaQuest* heat up as a result. With a replacement part not due for weeks, makeshift roommates are at each other's throats. Despite his better judgement suggesting otherwise, Captain Bridger calls on the one person who can help them: The Regulator.

Not known for his reputation as an upstanding businessman, he is combination junk man/pawn broker/enforcer. Standing over six feet tall and two hundred pounds, and clad in titanium boots and a weathered Marine duster, nobody is especially comfortable when he pays *seaQuest* a personal visit.

Except Lucas. To him The Regulator, and his sidekick orang-utan Verne, offer a welcome divergence from humdrum life on the vessel. But when Captain Bridger senses the computer whiz's admiration of The Regulator, he decides to fill the entire crew in on this peculiar character's past.

In the meantime, Verne discovers Darwin. When The Regulator goes to the Sea Deck to retrieve his partner, he is mesmerised upon hearing the dolphin talk. Given the trouble he tends to leave in his path, it is no surprise that when The Regulator finally leaves, *seaQuest* is not really rid of him. And it is not until Captain Bridger, Lucas and a security team seek him out in his lair, that we find out what The Regulator is really about.

The episode was written by David J. Burke and was directed by Les Sheldon.

"Sea West"

Off Australia's Great Barrier Reef, the *seaQuest*'s launch, with Bridger and crew aboard, arrives in answer to a distress signal from Broken Ridge, an undersea mining facility. It is the old west – circa 2018. The crew questions the pool players in the canteen and Ford is punched by Lenny Sutter, the miner who, they discover, sent the signal but must hide the fact from Deputy Cobb. Cobb arrives and breaks up the fight. Although Broken Ridge is a small town, it sits on an underwater mountain of gold. It is a difficult town to leave as Lenny and his family know. Cobb denies there was a distress signal and orders Bridger and the crew to leave. Lenny has the look of a condemned man under Cobb's scrutiny.

On their return to *seaQuest*, they find Banjo, Lenny's son's dog, with a message tucked under his collar which asks for help. With Bridger's approval, Hitchcock returns to Broken Ridge undercover as a singer, and immediately attracts Cobb. Flashing a stock of gold nuggets, he asks her to stay and marry him. Hitchcock avoids him long enough to find Lenny. He tells her that he and his family own the mine's mineral rights and ran the mines until Cobb led a takeover. Cobb shows up, attempts to beat information on Hitchcock out of Lenny, and is laid out by Hitchcock with a shovel.

Meanwhile, Bridger, Krieg and Ford return to town – via its back-door mine shafts – to rescue the Sutters. In the canteen, Hitchcock acts as a decoy by singing a sultry ballad to Cobb, who is entranced. Bridger arrives and saves the Sutter family as Krieg rushes to find Hitchcock. But Cobb spots him. He and Hitchcock run for their lives and reach the sea launch, but Cobb captures Ford. Bridger and the crew return for a showdown to Broken Ridge with Lenny, or risk Ford's life. The captain is armed with an ace-in-the-hole which may save all their lives and leave Cobb powerless with his ill-gotten gold.

The episode was written by John J. Sakmar and Kerry Lenhart, and was directed by Gabrielle Beaumont.

"Photon Bullet"

Captain Bridger is perplexed when the *seaQuest* receives an otherwise unexplained high security clearance UFO message instructing the vessel to immediately report to Node Three in order to deliver a routine part. An underwater communications installation, Node Three acts as a virtual central nervous system for any and all information sent via optic computer highways under the Pacific Ocean.

Upon arriving, Lucas meets Martin Clemens, the young, self-assured Node Three chief who oversees an even younger staff of élite computer hackers. It turns out to be somewhat of a vacation for Lucas, who, coincidentally, knows many of the Hackers from the hours he spends "on-line" communicating via electronic bulletin boards. Lucas soon learns that Clemens is one of his idols, a computer-hacking legend called "Mycroft". Lucas also enjoys his own notoriety as he learns that to the young hackers working at Node Three, Lucas, known in hacking circles as "Frankenstein", is a legend in his own right. The young computer expert especially enjoys the attention he receives from Julianna, aka "Red Menace", a young female hacker who is much more captivating in person than she ever was in cyber space.

And when he gets a peek inside the Node Three control room, a high-tech cacophony of blinking screens and sophisticated computer terminals operated by his on-line cohorts, Lucas is mesmerised by the power of its contents; the highest information density in the world. Coming at a time when the youngest member of the *seaQuest* crew is feeling constrained by the life of a submariner and resentful of *seaQuest*'s constant adult influences, Bridger lets Lucas stay at Node Three for a couple of days of R&R with his own contemporaries.

It's only after Bridger and the rest of the crew return to *seaQuest*, however, that Lucas learns that Node Three is much more than a reactive communications installation and that the hackers running this place aren't playing innocent computer games. Clemens' vitality as a leader may be blinding the young geniuses as they pursue Node Three's true objective. Lucas is caught between his admiration for Mycroft and his suspicions about Clemens. The real truth won't be revealed unless Lucas can win over his fellow hackers. In the end it's a battle of gigabytes as Mycroft and Frankenstein engage in a hacker's duel to the death. Only if Lucas wins will the true Clemens be revealed. And the lessons learned through Lucas's own actions force him to do more growing up than Captain Bridger ever would have imposed back on *seaQuest*.

The episode was written by David Kemper and was directed by Bryan Spicer.

"Better Than Martians"

The world waits with bated breath as the first manned mission to Mars, the *Wayfarer,* is scheduled to return to Earth. Manned by a four-man international crew, and commanded by one of Captain Bridger's closest friends from his days in the Navel Academy, the capsule is scheduled to return to Houston after a two-year round trip to the red planet.

In anticipation of the historic landing, the entire *seaQuest* crew is glued to the Earth Cast News broadcast – except Bridger and Dr Westphalen, who, despite their interest from a scientific perspective, are concerned about the political repercussions that the Mars Mission will almost certainly have on *seaQuest*'s funding.

But Bridger can ignore the event no longer when the capsule experiences problems re-entering the Earth's atmosphere, and uncontrollably plummets into the Andaman Sea. *SeaQuest* is the four astronauts' only hope for survival. As if lack of time is not enough of a hindrance, the Captain finds himself battling other forces, including territorial waters plagued by drug syndicates who are fighting a virtual war with the local confederation's government. Against his peaceful inclinations, Bridger is forced into storming towards the *Wayfarer* on full military alert.

But still, time is quickly running out for Bridger's long-time friend and professional nemesis. And when *seaQuest* experiences trouble reaching the astronauts, some critics, including the world's most powerful figures, wonder if Captain Bridger might have his own agenda. This development forces Bridger to come to terms with his conflicting feelings – the respect and love for a friend, and his adamant convictions on the importance of sea exploration *vis-à-vis* the space programme. In the end, only severe sacrifices in terms of his ship and his crew, will save the astronauts. But even then it might be too late.

The episode was written by David Kemper and Dan Brecher, and was directed by John T. Kretchmer.

"Nothing but the Truth"

Large contraptions attached to the *seaQuest* bulkhead are being tested – hull siphons that can refloat a sinking ship. Hitchcock and Ford confront each other, as the latter has been offered his own command away from the *seaQuest*. Suddenly, Bridger calls to have them rescue research scientists abroad a troubled deep-sea vessel. However, it proves to be Colonel Steven Schraeder, who appears with jump-suit armed commandos – the *seaQuest* faces an unexpected danger!

Schraeder, an environmentalist pushed over the edge, and his commandos demand the 'truth' to determine the power they gain with control of *seaQuest*. The commandos move through the boat in menacing precision. Hitchcock shuts down the boat's power systems before she is taken hostage – will she be able to deceive Schraeder and the commandos?

Krieg and Crocker struggle through air ducts to rescue the others with even Darwin trying to help. Lucas, escaping the commandos, joins Ford, and they battle the raiding enemy.

Ford and Bridger communicate and make counter plans, but will this cause the Captain to destroy his own boat? He knows Schraeder is a man dedicated to his principles but with tactics that threaten all mankind.

On the bridge it appears the *seaQuest* is sinking, the siphons disabled. Ford has blocked the intruders' escape, but Bridger must decide about storming the ship. Schraeder cannot be sure he is being told the truth when he decides to abandon ship. Who does he believe as he boards a submersible to escape?

The resulting conflict brings Ford to a new realisation about his role on the *seaQuest* as Bridger's second-in-command.

The episode was written by David Kemper and was directed by Les Sheldon.

"Greed for a Pirate's Dream"

The *seaQuest* hovers over the Therman Vent Platform. If the magna-buoy insertion works, man will be able to prevent volcanic eruptions and earthquakes.

Four months later on a tropical island, a dormant volcano belches, spitting out the buoy like a comet into the sky. At a treasure hunter's hovel, the charred buoy buries itself. The four inhabitants think the worse and take action to prevent being discovered.

Meanwhile, the *seaQuest* continues its journey. Captain Bridger and Lucas Wolenczak are preparing to go upworld to their Pearl Harbor, Honolulu base. Suddenly, there is a satellite secure alert, but Commander Ford has no time to get Bridger back. The screen maps show the Caribbean and pinpoint the supposedly uninhabited Monito Atoll. That, of course, becomes Ford's direction for the *seaQuest*.

Dr Raleigh Young, a leading government geologist, foresees a force of nature, a volcanic eruption, more devastating than a hydrogen bomb.

Back on the island, the treasure seekers' excavation pays off – but the UEO helicopters hover overhead in search of the buoy which is held by the hunters. A monitoring device leads the *seaQuest* and Ford to their location.

Retrieving the buoy, Ford cannot get the hunters to leave the island even if they are in imminent peril! Dr Young knows that another eruption can be expected that could blow up the entire area. The treasure seekers, not fully understanding the situation, refuse to abandon their long ambition. Suddenly, an explosion tears through the night – they have destroyed the *seaQuest* launch that brought Ford and Dr Young to the island.

Aboard the *seaQuest*, Bridger finds no launch communication response and knows something is very wrong as they receive serious seismic tremors from the Monito Atoll. Bridger and Dr Kristin Westphalen must make a dangerous decision to save those on the island facing death by the impending volcanic lava backwash.

The episode was written by David J. Burke and Robert Engels, and was directed by James A Contner.

"Whale Song"

Whaling ships are disappearing into thin air and the UEO suspects foul play. Captain Bridger is ordered by the Pentagon to hunt down the radical environmentalists who are out to save the whales – even at the expense of human life. But when Bridger's philosophies run counter to the UEO brass, he is faced with the most difficult decision of his life – resigning his command of the *SeaQuest,* or using deadly force to stop the aqua-vigilantes!

Bridger turns to home, as well as old friends, to help figure out how he might follow distasteful orders, without compromising his own values and selling out a comrade in arms. And with Lucas looking to learn from Bridger's actions, making the right decision is even more critical for the Captain.

The episode was written by Patrick Hasburgh and was directed by Bryan Spicer.

"The Stinger"

Off the coast of California, Captain Bridger and Commander Hitchcock hover from a Sea Crab as the sleek, one-seater Stinger, tail wagging like a fish, rockets by with Lucas Wolenczak at the controls. It's a prototype but tests appear a success. What they haven't counted on is Martin Tucker, on the surface in an outboard dinghy, monitoring the Stinger's path. Suddenly, a boom resonates, the Stinger is hit by something. There is radio silence from Lucas.

Bridger sends Ford, Krieg and Crocker on a rescue launch. However, Tucker leaves an almost unconscious Lucas on the seashore. It registers on the *seaQuest* and the launch goes for the rescue. Tucker has disappeared and so has the Stinger.

The loss of the Stinger is a security violation and a fierce "competition" swirls around its development. This includes the Hydrogear Labs, an Enzo Dinato Company, and his former engineer, Martin Tucker, whom Lucas recognises. Obviously, to find the Stinger they must find Tucker's workshop.

However, Hydrogear finds Tucker first and demands their property. Bringing Tucker to Dinato, who insists the former stay for qualifying runs of his prototype – but Tucker escapes.

Bridger's men locate Tucker and Crocker goes for him with a squad of men. When they arrive, Dinato's men are holding Tucker but Crocker takes command. They find the Stinger disassembled.

Bridger gives Lucas and Hitchcock orders to build another and the *seaQuest* crew join them. The Stinger will be in the UEO performance tests along with Tucker in his prototype.

In a fast-paced finale they challenge each other in a race with Lucas emerging with a lesson or two well learned.

The episode was written by John J. Sakmar, David J. Burke and Patrick Hasburgh, and was directed by Jonathan Sanger.

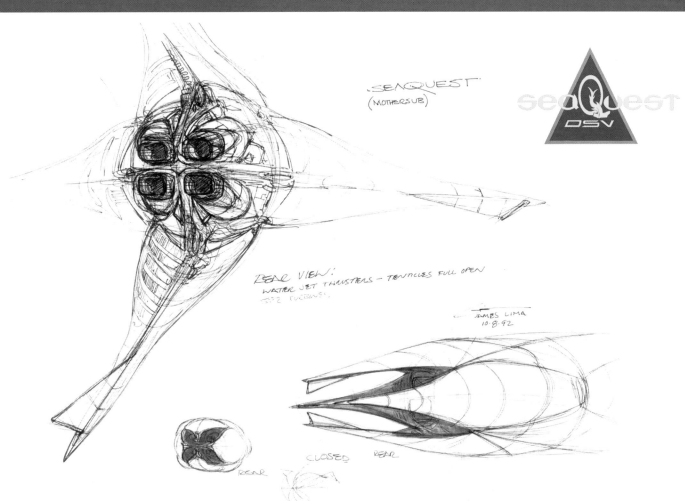

SEAQUEST
(MOTHERSUB)

seaQuest
DSV

REAR VIEW:
WATER JET THRUSTERS - TENTACLES FULL OPEN

JAMES LIMA
10.8.92

CLOSED   REAR

REAR

THE TECH SPECS

SeaQuest (DSV 4600)

Length:	1007 Ft.
Beam:	100 Ft.
Displacement:	31,700 Tons (SUBMERGED).
Propulsion:	Nuclear fusion-powered turbines (CLOSED SYSTEM).
Fuel:	Tritium (Eritium extracted from seawater).
Accommodations:	242 Total.
	88 Regular Navy/operational crew.
	124 Scientific personnel.
	20 Non-regular personnel.
Year design began:	2007
Year commissioned:	2013

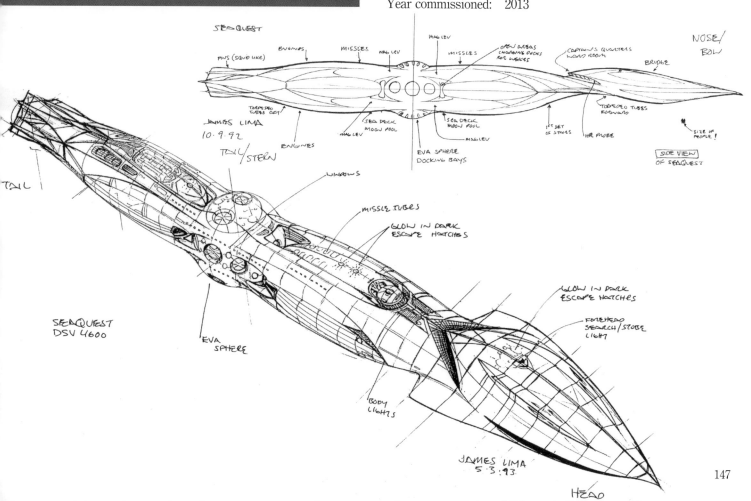

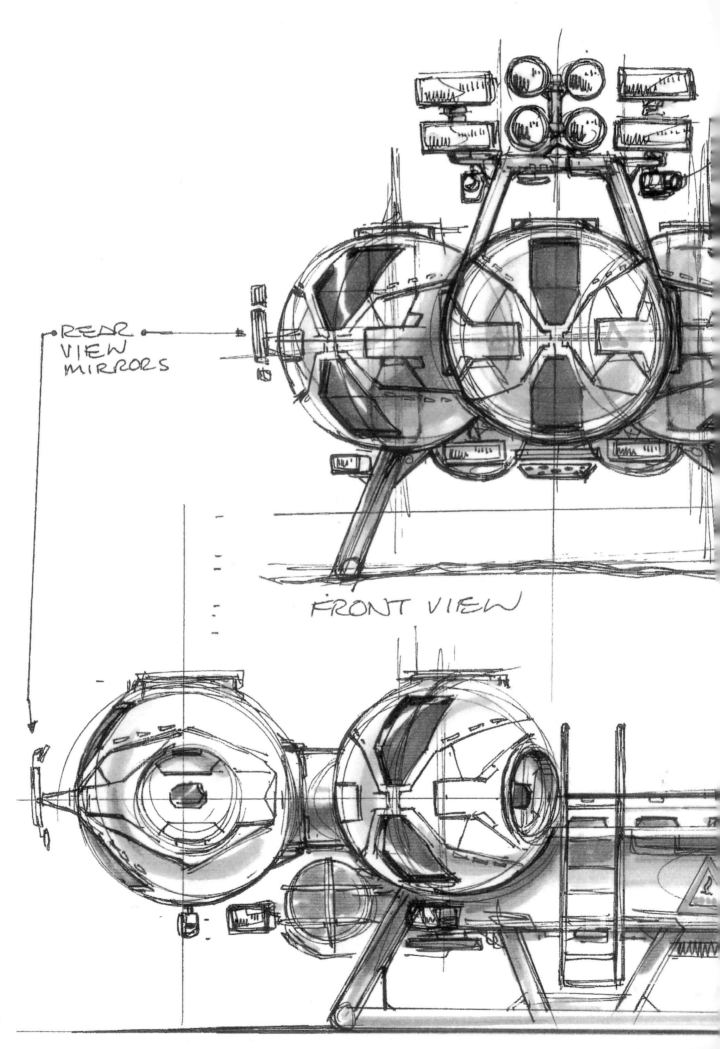

REAR
VIEW
MIRRORS

FRONT VIEW

— PANASONIC VIDEO CAMERAS – 360° VIEWING PLANE

"SEMI – TRUCK"
- 9 FOOT DIA. SPHERES
- 3 FOOT CONNECTION PORTALS

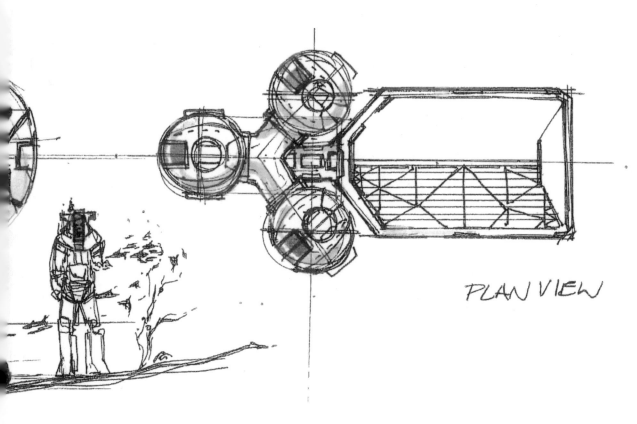

PLAN VIEW

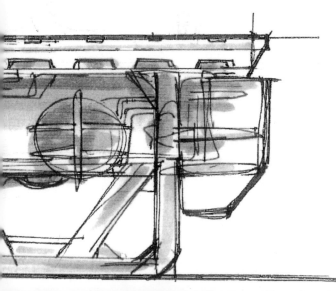

Deep Submergence Semi

Deep submergence semi's are the primary work vehicles of the ocean. They deliver massive loads to the sea floor for building and research. They can also be used as temporary housing for work crew and scientists. Poorer confederations have used these semi's as under-sea labs.

Operational to:	22,000 Ft.
Length:	61.6 Ft.
Beam:	18.1 Ft.
Displacement:	14,100 lbs.
Speed:	18 Knots.
On-board oxygen:	96 Hours.

Most models equipped with re-breathers.
Accommodations: N/A

Deep Submergence pick-up

Deep submergence pick-ups are derived from late twentieth-century technology. They are used by miners, farmers and explorers throughout the various confederations.

Operational to: 15,000 Ft.
Length: 35 Ft.
Beam: 14 Ft.
Displacement: 41,700 lbs.
Speed: 32 Knots.
On-board oxygen: 12 Hours.
Some models equipped with re-breathers.
Accommodations: N/A

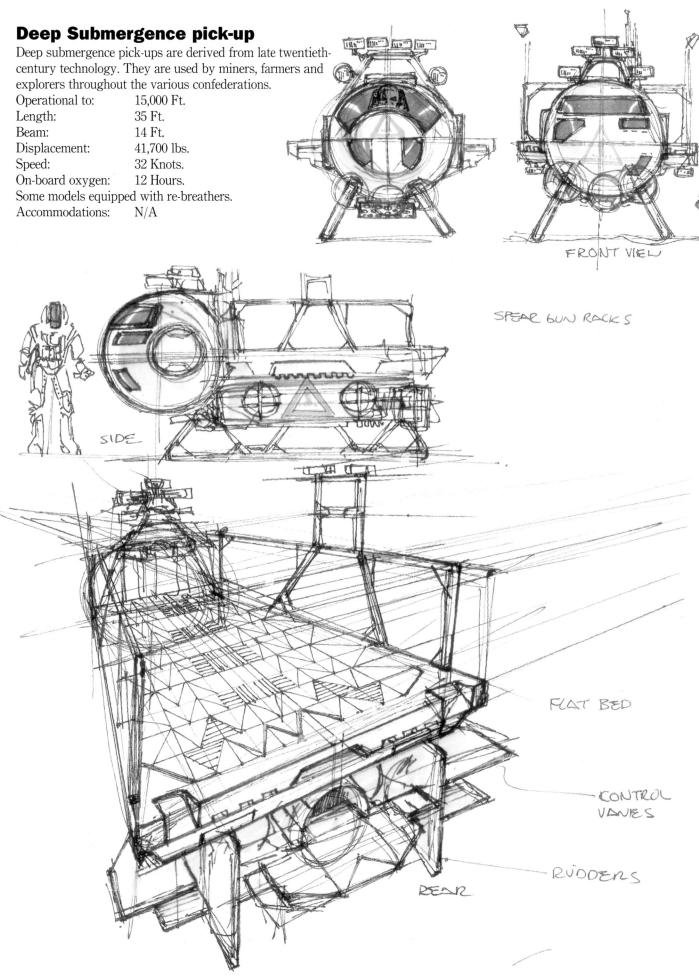

FRONT VIEW

SPEAR GUN RACKS

SIDE

FLAT BED

CONTROL VANES

RUDDERS

REAR

FRONT VIEW OF SHIELD/SEMI EVA SUIT

SPEEDER INTERIOR/COCKPIT

James Lima
7·17·92

Speeder

Modular high-speed recon craft designed for short-term
mission. This vehicle is able to change its configuration
whenever the mission requires.

Operational to: Classified.
Length: 61 Ft.
Beam: 18 Ft.
Displacement: 17,600 lbs.
Speed: Classified.
On-board oxygen: Classified.
Some models equipped with re-breathers.

Accommodations:

	Model		
	1	seats	6
	2		10
	3		14

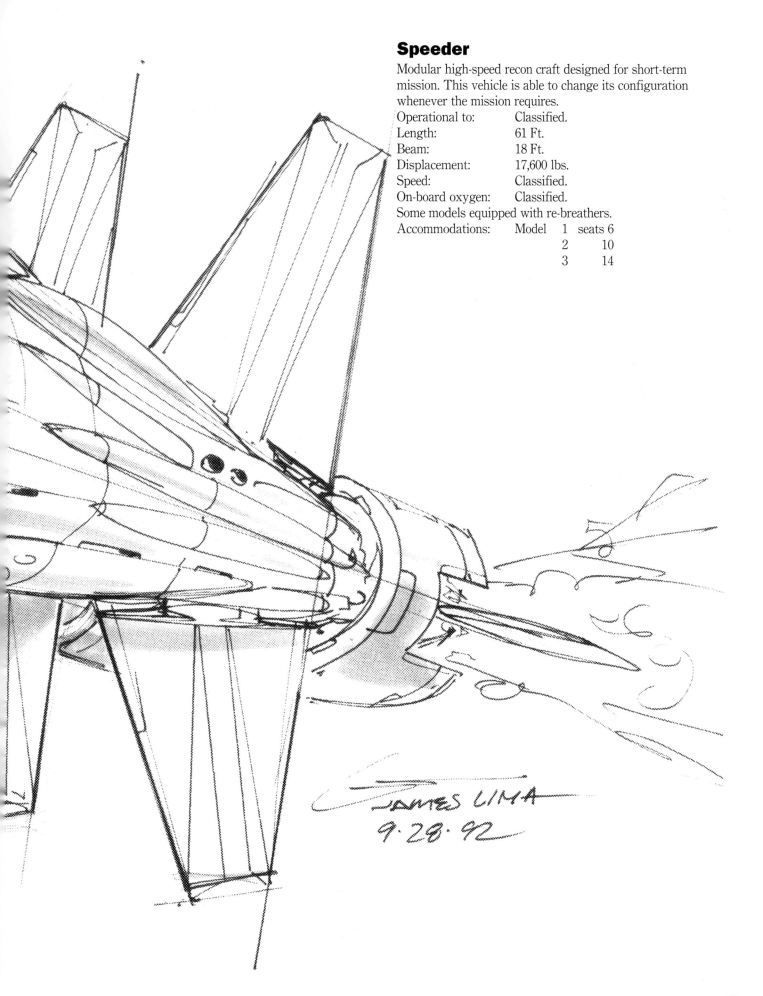

JAMES LIMA
9.28.92

Stinger

Stingers are single-pilot fast-attack craft deployed from *seaQuest*'s EVA ports located in the upper and lower docking ball.

Operational to:	25,000 Ft.
Length:	43.6 Ft.
Beam:	6.1 Ft.
Displacement:	31,681 lbs.
Speed:	Classified.
On board oxygen:	Tri-Helium mix and aqua return re-breathers units.
Weapons:	Mini-plasma torpedoes and electo-static arrays (stings).
Accommodations:	One.

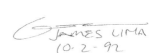

SIDE VIEW WINDOW THRU HEAD LIGHT COVER

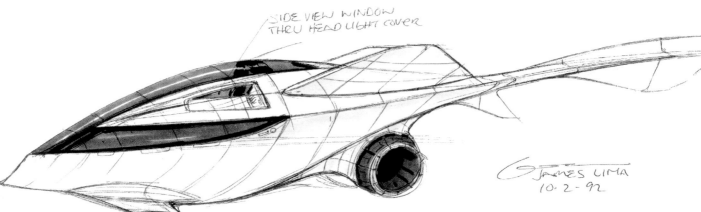

SIDE ELEVATION

JAMES LIMA

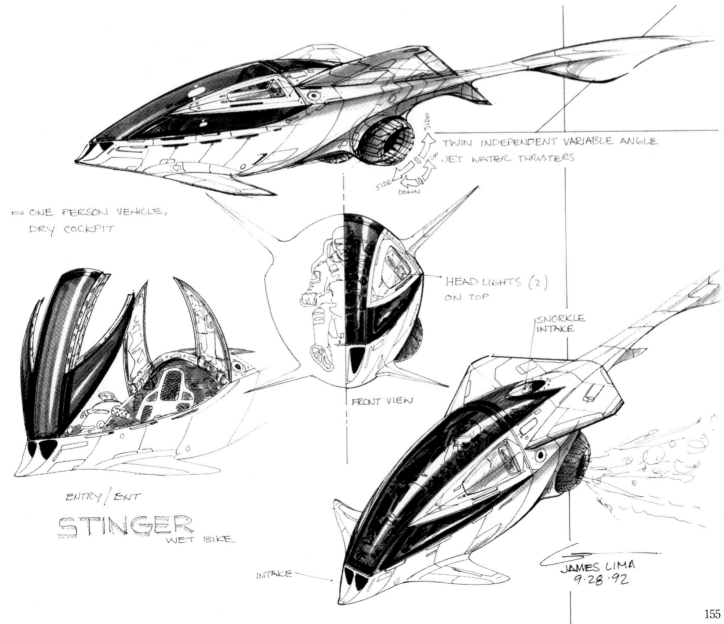

ONE PERSON VEHICLE,
DRY COCKPIT

TWIN INDEPENDENT VARIABLE ANGLE
JET WATER THRUSTERS

SIDE
UP
SIDE
DOWN

HEAD LIGHTS (2)
ON TOP

SNORKLE
INTAKE

FRONT VIEW

ENTRY / EXIT

STINGER
WET BIKE

INTAKE

JAMES LIMA
9.28.92

155

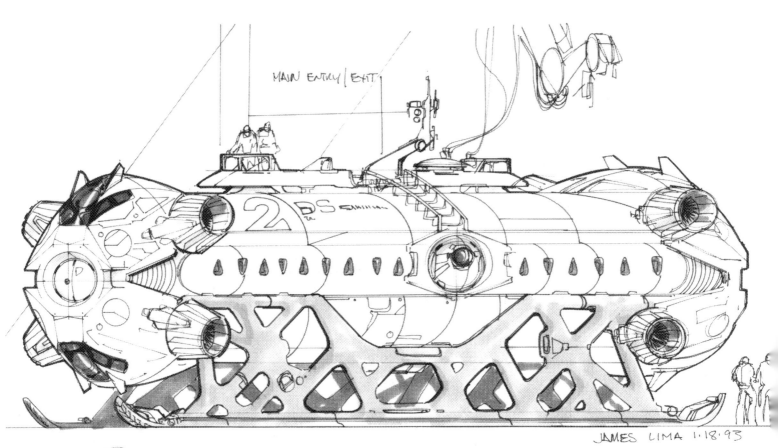

MAIN ENTRY/EXIT

2 DS

JAMES LIMA 1·18·93

sea Quest : "SHUTTLE CRAFT"

95ᵐ LONG

SHUTTLE CRAFT "CAB"

- EACH CAB CAN DETACH FROM PASSENGER MODULE

- ENTRY/EXIT/DOCKING UNIT

Sea Launch

DSV-46001-4 made of titanium capable of DSRD (Deep submergence rescue operations). Multi-purpose vehicle has a life support system capable of keeping 25 alive submerged to 10,000 ft. for 10 days. Universal
docking links enable this craft to attach itself to any vehicle or building under the sea.

Operational to:	10,000 Ft. (Normal)
Length:	66 Ft.
Beam:	Classified.
Displacement:	Classified.
Propulsion:	Nuclear fusion-powered turbines (CLOSED SYSTEM).
Fuel:	Tritium (Eritium extracted from seawater).
Accommodations:	25 Total.

WSKRS ("WHISKERS")

Wireless Sea Knowledge Retrieval Satellites. Spherical data-gathering probes. Sending back information on water temperature, currents, undersea obstruction, sea-life, etc. Acting somewhat like a cat's whiskers, they provide valuable data on the environment immediately surrounding the ship. They also are despatched to the surface, acting as the ship's periscope when necessary. WSKRS utilise video-imaging, sonar, as well as olfactory discrimination sensors which actually use a form of "smell" to better define objects in the inky blackness of the deep ocean.

21 available, 3 out at all times.

Operational to:	200 Metres surrounding the ship.
Length:	2 Metres.
Beam:	2 Metres.
Displacement:	Classified.
Propulsion:	Classified.

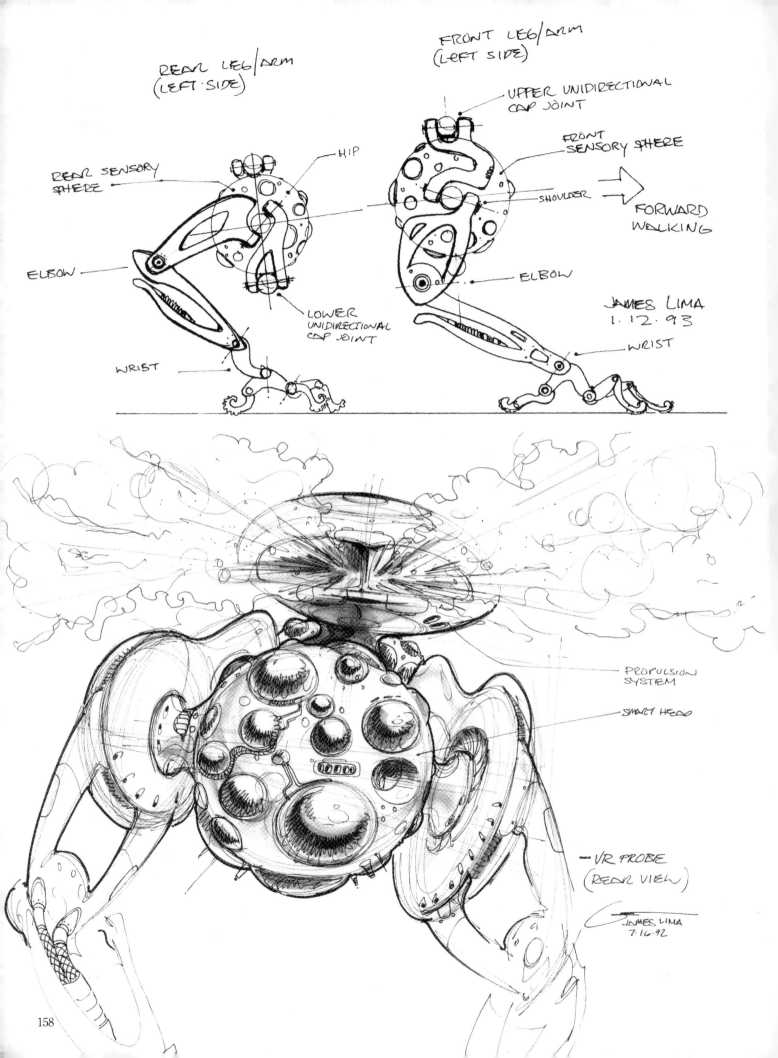

REAR LEG/ARM
(LEFT SIDE)

FRONT LEG/ARM
(LEFT SIDE)

UPPER UNIDIRECTIONAL
CAP JOINT

HIP

REAR SENSORY
SPHERE

FRONT
SENSORY SPHERE

ELBOW

SHOULDER

FORWARD
WALKING

ELBOW

JAMES LIMA
1.12.93

LOWER
UNIDIRECTIONAL
CAP JOINT

WRIST

WRIST

PROPULSION
SYSTEM

SMART HEAD

VR PROBE
(REAR VIEW)

JAMES LIMA
7.16.92

158

HR Probe

Highly sophisticated probe sled, capable of operating independent of the *seaQuest* up to a distance of 0.8 nautical miles. Compact size and mobility allow the HR probe to enter undersea caves, trenches, sunken ships, etc., that are otherwise inaccessible to exploration. Data relayed back to the ship provides the HR operator with a 360-degree "Virtual Reality" sight-and-sound rendering of whatever environment the HR probe is experiencing. Extendible probe "arms" allow for manual manipulation of the HR probe's environment by the HR operator on the ship.

Operational to: Classified.
Length: Classified.
Beam: Classified.
Displacement: Classified.
Propulsion: Classified.